Regency London

Douglas Hill

Picture sources: Radio Times Hulton Picture
Library pp. 16, 30, 33, 36, 44, 47, 51, 53, 56, 59,
61, 63, 72, 73, 79; Mansell Collection pp. 22, 76.
Photographs in centre section: London Museum
3, 7; Michael Taylor 1, 2, 4, 5, 6, 8. Guildhall
Museum slipcase illustration.

SBN 356 02568 3

© London Weekend Television Ltd., 1969
Macdonald & Co. (Publishers) Ltd.

First published in 1969 by
Macdonald & Co. (Publishers) Ltd.
St. Giles House, 49 Poland St., London W.1

Reprinted 1969

Made and printed in Great Britain by
Purnell & Sons Ltd., Paulton, Somerset

Discovering London 7

Regency London

Douglas Hill

Macdonald : London

Contents

Cover: A Bow Street Runner; more detectives than police-men. 'Runners' helped to reduce crime in late 18th-century London.
Slipcase illustration: Visscher's panorama of London, 1616.

Introduction

Historians love to attach labels to people and to periods. So the 77 years that are the subject of this book have come in for their share of such tags: the Age of Transition, the Age of Reform, the Age of Elegance (which is often applied to the whole 18th century), the Age of Revolution, and so on. Such catchy phrases are usually too neat to be entirely useful. The transitions, for instance, mostly had their beginnings earlier than 1760, and mostly went on developing after 1837. Besides, every separable period of history is transitional in its own way. Then, too, the reforms were indeed extensive, but they hardly swept the board of all the abuses and social evils that needed reforming. Nor did any one wave of reform ever build up without colliding with a rigid, powerful wall of conservatism. As for the elegance, it was the property of a tiny fraction of society, the upper segment. The rest of the world went on living in various degrees of ordinariness or downright squalor. Even the label 'Regency period', as used in this book's title, clouds as much as it defines: to be literal, the Prince did not become Regent until 1811, and then soon became king in his own right in 1820.

Perhaps if a label must be found, that of 'revolutionary' is the least misleading. During this period two of history's three greatest popular revolutions occurred—in America and in France—along with some less far-reaching revolts in more remote parts of the world, such as Spanish South America, and some definite restless stirrings and throne-topplings in nearly every other European nation and overseas colony. Simultaneously, new economic ideas and new technological processes were dragging the manufacturing nations into the disruptive modernity of the Industrial Revolution, while other new departures in agriculture were creating what is usually called the Agrarian Revolution. And, stimulated by these virtual hurricanes of change, a number of clear thinkers and a number of high-powered demagogues (often one and the same) began looking searchingly at the underpinnings of the traditional social structure and pronouncing many of them rotten. Revolutionary ideas like that of human rights and social equality gained currency; humanitarian movements gained followers. Science and medicine, too, exploded into a flurry of breakthroughs; art and especially poetry became *avant-garde* for the first time in British history, in a clean break with tradition.

But of course where there is revolution there is always counter-revolution. The British fought desperately to put down the breakaway Americans, and also fought the French. Napoleon rose to turn a republic into an empire. Reactionaries of every breed sneered at the new art and science, balked the proposed changes in economic and social patterns, and brought their biggest guns into action against the possibility of political advance. So the age of revolution turns out to be just as much the age of ambivalence, of contradictions, of one step forward and two or three back. Yet in the process, during those steps forward, a great deal of groundwork was laid in all social and economic spheres for the world that we live in now.

7

The Changing World

George III, 22 years old, with manic depressive tendencies, mounted the throne in 1760 as the first of the 18th-century Georges to be oriented wholly towards Britain (as opposed to Hanover). He had need to be: cracks were radiating all across the smooth face of that century's notable stability and calm. It was George's misfortune to be determined to rule, to dominate his government, at a time when the structure of political power as his predecessors had known it was about to suffer drastic overhauling and alteration. Similar upheavals were to be felt in the social and economic patterns of the nation—the patterns that had led the 18th century, the 'Augustan Age', to proclaim itself as having reached the very peak of civilisation.

Hindsight lets us see one of the first signals of future changes in a growing dissatisfaction with politics. The political system was still very much factional—which meant that power was held by small groups of men, each dominated by a strong leader, quite irrespective of party allegiances. Party politics as we know it hardly existed.

The king appointed to power whatever ministers he felt could control Parliament and run the country. (Public opinion, though mattering, was a secondary consideration at most.) Throughout the century the Whig party had dominated—but this meant that when one great Whig nobleman and his clique had power, his most dangerous opponents would be other power-hungry Whigs. The Tories, with their share of aristocrats but mainly a party of smaller landowners with many links among the wealthy urban middle classes, languished in the political wilderness.

So politics meant a series of jostlings for power and for the king's favour among several great Whigs and their groups. And there was no longer a Walpole to hold the country together for years, strong and secure in his position. Insecurity was rife among ministers, through the 1760s and long after, as men like the dominating elder Pitt, the great manipulator Newcastle, the liberal Charles James Fox and a host of lesser men played a kind of political musical chairs in their governmental intrigues and manoeuvres. None of the insecurity was diminished by the king's continuing attempts to maintain his own power within the tangle of alliances and conflicts—and in spite of his increasing mental instability.

Socially and economically, too, the massive 18th-century stasis began to show some slight tremors. Britain remained in the 1760s an agricultural nation, where social as well as political leadership was vested in the landed aristocracy, where by far the majority of people lived in small towns or rural villages with the local lord or squire as the ultimate authority. Hindsight, again, shows the potential disruptions beneath the surface, already at work undermining the traditional order of affairs. New ideas about farming—especially about the enclosure of common land—had begun to spring up here and there around the country. These were isolated outbreaks mostly, not yet signifying an epidemic; yet they were significant. So were the parallel novelties in the business of manufacturing—again in particular areas such as the textile-producing north, but spreading, and spelling the beginning of the end for the economic dominance of the landlords.

In 1760 Britain was at war with France, as she had been desultorily, off and on, throughout the century. Mostly these wars ended with treaties that contained a series of clever diplomatic exchanges, rather as in chess, of overseas and European possessions. British eyes had been gazing abroad for years by this time, and her involvements were growing as her imperial urge (and sea-power) began to burgeon. The eastern seaboard of America was hers; so were good-sized portions of the West Indies. Both meant quantities of produce that could be used (apart from domestic uses) in the international trade and mercantilism at which Britain had become expert. Every bit as much a trading nation as an agricultural one, Britain looked on delightedly as the East India Company consolidated its power in India (thanks to Clive's successes there); and no one minded that the Company had in itself become virtually a separate colonial power. But soon unwise speculation, internal corruption and frequent localised wars in the sub-continent began to weaken the Company—and in the 1770s Britain abandoned her usual preference for mercantilism before colonialism, and brought India under partial control of the crown. So brand-new problems of empire began to beset her, bringing new insecurities in their wake.

Towards Parliamentary Reform

None of the stirrings of a new order mentioned so far could have indicated to men of the time that their country (and the world) was hurtling towards a period of disorder, unrest and sudden change. Most authorities agree that perhaps the earliest clear storm warning came from the rise of a popular movement towards reform of Parliament. Naturally, in that time of intrigue, the political leaders manipulated the House of Commons however they could—by means of patronage and jobbery, bargains with local squires whose tenants voted (in far from secret ballots) as they were told, even outright bribery. The worst abuses of the parliamentary system occurred during elections in the boroughs, more numerous and returning more MPs than the rural county constituencies. The vote was awarded haphazardly— usually to householders with property above a certain value, but never consistent through the nation. And there were the infamous 'rotten' boroughs, where a mere handful of electors in each had the right to put two MPs into the House—and so could hardly avoid corruption. All the while, the growing manufacturing towns like Manchester or Leeds remained unrepresented, because parliamentary representation had not been updated since the days of Charles II.

But in London the electorate was too big to be bribed, the national policies and events were of instant local importance, the wealthy City men resented the long shadows cast by the Whig peers, and the City itself had access for its pressure groups to both king and Commons. So it was in London that a reforming spirit caught fire, and the agitation for a new look at Parliament began. It found a figurehead in a rabble-rousing journalist and sometime MP named John Wilkes, whose uninhibited attacks on the 'King's party' led to his being charged with seditious libel. He fled the country, and while absent was expelled from Parliament. In 1768 he returned, stood in a Middlesex election, won—and was promptly expelled again. He repeated this process several times, to the point of farce, while his supporters increased; then the exasperated government declared one of his unsuccessful opponents to be the duly elected member. The

Wilkesians rose in riot, and much of London joined them.

Whether Wilkes deserved expulsion or not, the election was plainly and openly being manipulated in direct opposition to the will of the electorate. The riots died down, but the agitation went on—expanding into demands for an extended and clarified franchise, reorganisation of constituencies, an end to the rotten boroughs. Wilkes had awakened the people (largely inadvertently) to a consciousness of their constitutional rights, in direct conflict with the entrenched Whig government and the 'ruling class' from which its members came.

Not that Britain was hovering on the brink of actual revolution. The issue of parliamentary reform was to go on burning for nearly two generations before it was resolved. In the meantime other sources of instability had made their appearance, diffusing the unrest. Ministerial changes continued, as no one man seemed powerful enough to take hold of the country, to create a workable foreign policy or control a domestic one. No one was happy with the Peace of Paris in 1763 that ended the Seven Years' War: it was thought a mistake, for instance, to keep Canada while giving back to the French the West Indian sugar island of Guadeloupe. British finances were in trouble after the war, which meant more taxes— direct taxation, in those days before income tax, and imposed, as today, on the people's small luxuries. Beer already bore a tax, so the government imposed their demands on cider and wine. That brought wild rioting all across the south of England (the 18th-century propensity for rioting as an expression of political feeling makes our modern radical demonstrations look fairly pale). London issued some snappish petitions to the king. The cider tax was hastily dropped, which did not lend a great deal of credibility to the government's authority. By then some equally ill-advised fund raising had angered another set of anti-authoritarians: the American colonists.

The American Colonies

In the mid-1760s the colonies were contributing to the Exchequer in a variety of indirect ways, mostly through duties and tariffs. Then they received the blow of a direct tax: a stamp duty (taxing all official papers). The disgruntled colonists echoed a cry that had begun to be heard in the new towns of Britain's industrial north: 'no taxation without representation'. A quick political compromise repealed the Stamp Act, while declaring Britain's right to tax colonies (so saving face). But the unappeased Americans switched their opposition to a 1766 Act whereby the British military authorities could commandeer bed and board for troops in the colonies. Then the British government, irritated by the colonial intransigence and still harried by money troubles, imposed in 1767 a host of new customs duties.

Trouble was bound to come—the more so because of the unusual undercurrents of American life, its special forms of individualism and self-sufficiency, fed by puritanism and the demands of frontier survival. This ambiance led naturally to a dislike of overseas interference, and rebelliousness against anything resembling economic exploitation by remote, lordly England. So the colonists reacted by refusing to import English goods. Soon most of the duties had been taken off—except for that on tea—but before the Americans had heard of these relaxations a group of Bostonians had provoked some British troops into battle. Five Americans were shot and killed in this 'Boston Massacre'—which gave new purpose to the hard-core revolutionaries.

Then in 1773 Britain tried to offload some surplus tea onto the colony, while demanding the duty. The Boston radicals promptly staged their famous Tea Party. Britain retaliated by closing the port of Boston. At this point the Quebec Act, aimed to regulate the administration of Canada, seemed to declare the great frontier wilderness of Ohio out of bounds to Americans. More recruits joined the rebels-to-be. Britain, failing to grasp all the issues and their causes, tried at once to retaliate and conciliate. The colonial militia armed itself; British troops tried to confiscate the arms; shots were fired at Lexington, and theoretically were heard round the world. Britain set out to crush the rebels in one of the least inspired and most poorly organised wars she had ever fought.

Six years later Washington's ragged, half-starved militia and their French allies had won. The birth of the U.S.A. surely marks the final death of the old 18th-century order. The American War of Independence helped to focus and concretise a great many of the amorphous new concepts that were disturbing the world. The Declaration of Independence contained such radical new departures as an assertion of the 'rights of man'. And the world's first written constitution gave strength and substance to the embryonic spirits of democracy and republicanism.

The Growth of Liberalism

In the 1770s the British liberals and radicals had been finding their voices in many areas. The continuing groundswell of demand for parliamentary reform had spread further through the land, and was attracting more and more respectable men to its banner. It was now adding more idealistic demands—as for universal male suffrage, or annual parliaments—to its platform. Even so, liberalism was as yet a fairly small-time movement in Britain, and ran into many setbacks. For instance, the growing humanitarianism (to be discussed again later), expressing its distaste for the exploitation of the Indians in India, may well have contributed as much as political intrigue to the impeachment in 1785 of Warren Hastings, the dictatorial though reasonably successful expansionist governor-general of the colony. That controversy lasted

Troops quelling the Gordon Riots in 1780; these violent anti-Catholic demonstrations were partly provoked by animosity against immigrant Irish labourers.

seven years, and severely widened the gulfs between political extremes, especially after Hastings won his case. Earlier, the new order had lost again when a spirit of religious tolerance—intended for Roman Catholics—backfired into violent protesting on the part of extremist Protestants. (Extra ammunition for the anti-Catholics came from the unrest in Ireland, which was chronic throughout the whole late Georgian period and longer.) Not even the titular leader of the anti-Catholics, Lord George Gordon, had expected the wild nights of violence and burning that swept through the London streets in the so-called Gordon riots.

These setbacks showed, perhaps, that British reform-ism was not to be a sudden, sweeping, overall movement, but fragmented and particularised. And they warned against the inevitability of a grass-roots reaction against any changes imposed from above, or any too rapid changes. At the same time, the liberal elements were also Englishmen, and products of the great age of reason, believing (if their beliefs can be generalised) that change must come, but through the proper processes and chan-nels, without recourse to civil disorder. (The rise to prominence of the younger Pitt, with a good deal of reformist thinking in his policies, drained off some of the liberals' fire.) Few of their number rallied to the radical-ism of Tom Paine, or joined the smaller groups that muttered to themselves the grand, rolling phrases of Jeffersonian democracy. The broad front of radicalism in the 1780s shied away from thoughts of armed, bloody revolt. Instead, that kind of revolution took place across the channel.

The French Revolution and Napoleon

At first the French Revolution gave some impetus to the scattered reform movements of Britain, and liberal thinkers rose to praise its libertarian, egalitarian and fraternal ideals (while at the same time reserving a few doubts about the amount of blood spilled). Then, as Revolution gave way to Terror, as the evil word 'republicanism' began to be shouted across the channel at George III, reaction set in. The popular mood underwent a conservative and royalist backlash—fostered partly by unjustified fears of a popular revolt among England's masses. British liberalism and reformism were felt to be tainted by association. Radical societies virtually went underground in the face of witch-hunts, government informers and the threat of new laws against sedition. And the backlash reached new heights in 1793, when Pitt led the country to war against republican France.

Britain had hoped for a short war, in which her rapidly growing navy would win overseas bargaining counters. But these hopes were thwarted, principally by the rise of Napoleon through the ranks of the French army into leadership of his country. The war opened wide during the 1790s; Britain faced setbacks, the loss of allies, the threat of invasion. By 1800 Britain stood alone against the overrun Europe of France's new First Consul. To make matters worse, an offshoot of the European war broke out in India, and Britain faced the choice of making the subcontinent wholly subject to the crown by force of arms, or abandoning it to the French. Governor-General Wellesley (with the help of his brother, who was to become the Duke of Wellington) subdued India; meanwhile some of the principles of the French Revolution had found willing listeners among the doubly oppressed Catholic poor of Ireland. Rebellion threatened in that island, with the added fear that France might use disaffected Irishmen for its own warlike purposes. Fighting broke out in Ireland in 1798; the rising was ruthlessly crushed by British troops, and an Act of Union (ending the Irish parliament, giving Ireland representation at Westminster) tried to paper over the remaining cracks. Pitt set out to follow it with legislation for Catholic emancipation, but neither king nor country was yet ready for it, and Pitt lost power.

By this time (1802) Britain was growing desperate— with food shortages, financial difficulties, the terrible drain of the war effort. The new government took its first chance to negotiate a peace, though it meant giving up most of Britain's conquests while France kept many of hers. But it was an uneasy peace, and short-lived: Napoleon's expansionist ambitions led to war again in 1803, and war brought Pitt back to power. This time it was to be a defensive war, allowing Napoleon to rampage through Europe while ensuring that the British Navy now truly ruled the seas. Trade (including the slave trade to the West Indies) had made Britain a great maritime nation in the 18th century; now, at the outset of the 19th, war made her the greatest. The Navy spread its resources in a thin line from the Caribbean to the Baltic, to blockade Europe and to strike at the French fleet. And it proved its greatness in 1805 with Nelson's shattering victory at Trafalgar.

But Napoleon had of course consolidated his victories on land, and by 1811 had spread himself across Europe and was threatening Russia. It seemed almost anticlimactic that George III should choose that year to slip permanently into the insanity to which he had always been prone. So the over-weight, affable, extravagant and dissolute Prince of Wales became Regent. And, though this change had no part in it, the war took a turn for the better—as Napoleon's vast army foundered on a Russian winter, and as Wellington began to storm through Spain. Not even the entry of America into the war against Britain, stretching the Navy's resources still further, could alter the fact that the end was near. Soon the Russians were pouring into Germany, Wellington was crossing the Pyrenees. In 1814 Napoleon capitulated.

In 1815, as everyone knows, he attempted a comeback in the terrible One Hundred Days before Waterloo.

Afterwards, peace settled unfamiliarly on Europe; crowned heads reappeared, and thrones were remade for them. In some ways the old pre-revolutionary days returned, but not entirely—for too many people had got a brief scent of ideals like equality and human rights. And, in Britain, propaganda about British 'liberty' (as opposed to Napoleonic 'tyranny') had given the masses a taste for it. Where France's revolution had spawned a conservative backlash in Britain, France's empire—and the rapid, far-reaching changes that war had brought—had given new life to radicalism and liberalism.

The Industrial Revolution

Before 1790, as was indicated earlier, that great change which later generations would call the Industrial Revolution was apparent only in embryo. Certain technological advances in textiles—the spinning jenny and others—had appeared, but their use spread slowly; equally slow was the gradual drawing together of individual artisans, under the umbrella of factory-owning capitalism that took buying and selling out of their hands, turning them into wage-earners. But then the advent in the 1780s of steam power (in the engines of James Watt) and the advent of war and its economic necessities stepped up the progress of industry. Iron and steel production expanded geometrically: the many new iron bridges in the 1790s were only one indication of the abundance and relative cheapness of the metal. The comparatively young cotton manufacturing industry boomed, and the new power loom took weaving out of the artisans' cottages and put it into steam-powered factories. The industrial towns began to swell: Manchester doubled its population (to 100,000) from 1790 to 1815. Even the old established wool industry embraced new processes, and speeded production in time to profit from the new Australian source of raw material after 1815. The

Staffordshire potteries, following Josiah Wedgwood's lead, centralised the factories and imposed mass-production methods. With the increase in the use of steam, coal became all-important, and the mining industry blossomed into a major factor of the economic boom.

In this way England was transformed from a great trading nation into a great industrial (or producing) nation. Exports rose steeply, and the ship-building industry was as hard-pressed by merchant marine demands as formerly by the Navy's. Domestic transport improved as well: Britain's appalling roads underwent sudden and extensive improvement (as will be indicated in the next chapter); canal building entered a hectic phase, of vital importance to London as the main clearing house for raw materials entering the country and finished goods leaving it. And in what seems a very short time the stationary steam engines of the new factories experienced a translation that gave them wheels, and tracks to run on. The Victorian railway age had its roots in the Regency.

Improved transport, and increased factory production, both speeding the growth of the industrial towns, wreaked havoc on the agricultural world: revolutionary techniques and attitudes wreaked more. New seeding processes and ideas of fertilising, crop rotation and more were taking their toll on the traditionally tiny farms of open fields inefficiently tilled. But agriculture remained central to the British economy even when industry was reaching new heights in the 1790s, and more so in wartime when imports were always in jeopardy. Efficiency had to be imposed, which meant larger units and enclosed fields, as well as better methods of cultivation. The effects of this change were hard on the smallholder barely paying his way, and disastrous for the cottager working common land—who became merely a labourer on the new private farms, or who often gave up and sought work in the towns.

Town life, too, faced changes for the worse. Some of

A cartoon of a meeting (in 1796) to protest against a measure to curb 'seditious' reformist movements after the French Revolution.

these will be discussed in the next chapter, but can be hinted at here in everything implied by the ideas of overcrowding, filth, jerry-built houses and (however much it sounds like a communist slogan) systematic exploitation of the working people. The last is perhaps nowhere so obvious as in the transportation of pauper children from their homes to northern industrial towns, as indentured labour for the factories. But, as the abuses and social evils grew, so did the spirit of humanitarianism (if not, perhaps, in equal measure). Reformers and philanthropists sprang into crusades, to increase education, to correct the horrors of prisons and asylums, to improve the lot of the poor, to protect child labourers. If many of their efforts failed, or accomplished only minute parts of the improvement that was necessary, this perhaps is always the case with reform movements, which are curative rather than preventative—like a man baling an open boat in a storm. At least the reformers could take heart from a few notable successes, such as the fight for the abolition of the slave trade that began in the 1780s and was won (largely by the heroic parliamentary battles of Pitt's friend Wilberforce) in 1807. If nothing else, the humanitarians were awakening the British upper classes to an awareness of the squalor and misery around them, to which they had been entirely blind for centuries.

Soceity in flux

The bright new spirit of liberalism and reform stayed very much alive after 1815, but had just as hard a time trying to catch up with the continuing acceleration of social change. Much of the difficulty came from the conservative backlash mentioned before, as the opponents of change clung to outmoded or even long-dead ways while also clinging to the reins of power. They gained added strength when the liberal cries for a brave new post-war world verged on extremism, and when the unsettling novelties and restlessness of the time began to frighten the solid English citizen.

Part of the social chaos stemmed from the absence of solidity at the top. The Prince Regent's scandalous life —muddied by debts, dubious mistresses and the unceremonious dumping of his queen, Caroline (who became briefly a popular heroine in spite of her own well-known profligacy)—made him odious to the people. Nor did his reputation improve when he finally became king upon the death of George III in 1819. Royalty was never in such disrepute; and this fact led political radicals to talk of republicanism, than which nothing could have driven traditionalists further into their entrenched opposition.

The position of the arts clearly reflects the deepening split between these extremes—a split that has remained very familiar to us, in our own unsettled century of hectic transition and change. Where 18th-century writers and artists had remained firmly embedded in their society, faithfully reflecting its virtues and satirising its vices, the new artists formed an *avant-garde* that consciously accepted and broadcast a world-view far different from that of the citizenry. The painter Turner undermined the formalism of 18th-century art; the poets Wordsworth and Coleridge employed fresh forms and techniques, wrote of the need for passion and spontaneity in poetry, and turned their backs on man as he was, to write of nature and man as he should be. And they were scorned and attacked, as much as any 20th-century 'experimental' poet has been, for being obscure, silly and anti-poetic.

The traditionalist forces applied more serious weapons than scorn to the crucial issues of the time—those of politics. Radicals and progressives rightly believed that the reform of parliament, of the legislators, should be the first target. A more representative government would make the adoption of popular demands for reform much easier. But the very idea of 'popular demands' called up in the minds of the ruling classes the bogey of the French Revolution with its attendant nightmares of violence, republicanism and anarchy. The war, combined with the usual ministerial factionalism and intrigue, had brought the downfall of the Whig leaders about 1807; the Tories had gained power then, and were to hold it until 1830. But true party politics had still not developed; the change meant, largely, that because the Tories now had a majority in the Commons both the ruling faction and the opposition factions would be composed of Tories. In short, now that peace had diminished the need for unity in politics, government was as riddled with corruption and manoeuvring as it had ever been in the 1760s.

This state of affairs brought more clear-headed men onto the bandwagon of reform. And public opinion closed firmly behind it after a few administrative excesses, such as the vastly unpopular Corn Laws after the war, or the repressive laws against 'sedition' that were passed after a rise in unemployment brought a wave of riots and strikes. Those laws were toughened further after some extremist hurled stones at the Regent in 1816, and after a wild demonstration in 1819 (against the prohibition of mass meetings) panicked the authorities into ordering the troops to open fire—the 'Peterloo Massacre', in which many demonstrators were killed and hundreds wounded. So the closed circle continued to spin: reformist agitation leading to repressive reaction leading to a closing of the ranks of the reformers, and so on. Finally towards the end of the 1820s the Tory party fell apart as the Whigs had before them. The Duke of Wellington tried to hold the government together for a while, but most Englishmen could now see how desperately overdue was the hoped-for revision of the country's political structure.

When new (and mostly bloodless) revolutions in 1830

started toppling ancient thrones in France and elsewhere in Europe, the British rulers hastily bowed to the inevitable. New elections restored the Whigs to power, pledged to reformist policies. By 1832 a Reform Bill had been enacted that expanded and redistributed constituencies, finishing off the rotten boroughs and succeeding in creating a House of Commons far more representative of broad public opinion than the country had ever seen. It was still far from democratic: little improvement had been made in the franchise, and the ballot was still open (leaving voters corruptible). But certainly a major breach in the sea-wall of conservatism had been made—allowing for further social reforms to be introduced with a minimum of fuss, such as the belated abolition of slavery throughout the Empire.

The revolutions in Europe and the crises of reform in Britain (including riots enough during the arguments over the Reform Bill to breed fears of civil war) considerably overshadowed the death of George IV in 1830, which brought to an end the lengthy Georgian period of English history. The seven-year reign of the dull, inept but not unpopular William IV was something of an interregnum. The stormy atmosphere relaxed somewhat in the 1830s: liberalism had won a great battle, and had in the process strengthened itself to go on fighting its war. And, also, it had managed neatly to round off the 'age of revolution' with a closed circle, resolving the political issue with which the age had opened so frenetically in the 1760s.

Unquestionably, Britain had had its revolution just like so many other nations. But British revolutions seem usually to be gradual occurrences, evolutions, marred by many false starts and retrenchments, gathering impetus slowly over generations. The popular movements towards democracy, egalitarianism and social reform that got under way in the late Georgian era went on long after 1837. They may be going on still.

Life of the City

The City's growth

The dramatic expansion of London that took place in the late Georgian period grew partly out of a general increase in the population of the country, and partly out of the new but growing migration of workers to the cities. In 1760 England and Wales had a combined population of slightly more than six million (and a high death rate had kept increases gradual), and London held about 700,000. Bristol was the second city, trailing far behind at 50,000; no other towns came near this mark. By 1812 the British people numbered nearly 12 million, and more than a million of them were Londoners—with Edinburgh, Glasgow, Manchester, Birmingham and Liverpool well ahead of Bristol, and Leeds crowding close behind. By the 1830s these cities had leapt ahead even more sensationally: Leeds held 53,000 people in 1801, 120,000 in 1831.

London did not spread physically on all fronts, like concentric ripples on water, but in specific clumps—stretching out along a main road in one place, leaping over fields to build an estate development in another. As the next chapter will show, the principal directions of expansion were west and north. Since at least the 17th century, the fashionable area of London had been shifting westwards, away from the City that was more and more becoming the dividing line between the poor East End and the well-to-do West End. The Strand and Charing Cross areas, then Westminster, then the first signs of new fashionableness in Mayfair and Marylebone —these were the growth areas for the moneyed Londoners. East and south-east London were growing too, in fact mushrooming, but to a great extent in labyrinths of narrow streets, alleys and courts, clogged with squalid houses and tenements and their overcrowded residents, spreading like a stain on both sides of the river—all this over an area where grand country houses had stood in the 17th century. Because the nearness of this poor area had its effects on the City, substantial men who went to business in that commercial centre preferred to live outside it. Their favoured growth area for comfortable, garden-surrounded homes seemed to be the northeast—so that Islington quickly became an attractive suburb of London and areas to the north of that had their first tastes of being what we would call 'ex-urban'.

Such new areas, as has been said, would largely be linked to the main body of the city by thin lines of population, usually shops and houses straggling along the main road. So open spaces remained plentiful, even during the period of tremendous growth, surprisingly near the city's heartland—such as the fields east of Tottenham Court Road, or the Tothill Fields in Westminster, or Moorfields in the City, or Lincoln's Inn Fields. Not that all of these spaces had much in common with the greenness and pleasantness of the idealised countryside: they were often dumping grounds for refuse of all kinds, and stamping grounds for rough elements (Tothill Fields was one of the last places in the early 19th century where bull-baiting still went on). For more pleasant open spaces, one had to seek out the great parks of London, or be wealthy enough to have fine gardens around your West End home—or walk into the country. Fortunately, that walk was not a long one, even in the 1820s. By then many satellite villages had been swallowed by the expanding city (such as Kensington or Hackney), but places as near as Kentish Town were still separate villages with farmland between them and the city—and places like Hampstead, Dulwich or Chiswick were decidedly in the country, good retreats for Romantic poets to live in or City businessmen to escape to for weekends.

London's Transport

The reign of George III was the last age of coaching, before the railways got going. The wealthy moved around the country in their coaches or carriages, and the ordinary people who avoided horseback travelled in the great lumbering stage-coaches—which became both larger and more manageable as the period progressed. By the turn of the century and after, a stage-coach could carry a passenger 90 miles in not much more than 15 hours, including stops for three meals. And at the same time the cost of travelling had been reduced, in these larger vehicles, by the addition of outside seats on top of the coach—where passengers risked rain and chill to save on fares.

Poorer people might travel by stage-wagon, cheaper but vastly slower than coaches—or, more likely, they walked. Men in a hurry might travel by the fast and reliable mail-coach, when they did not ride their own horses. Certainly horseback was the surest means of getting anywhere on British roads at the time: the depth of the ruts, the stickiness of the mud, and the sheer volume of traffic (not to mention the proliferation of highwaymen in the 18th century) could make coach travel frustrating,

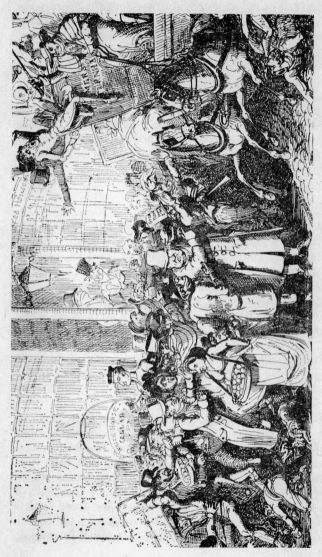

Piccadilly in 1825. London streets were a mêlée of pedestrians, wagons, coaches and carriages, all jostling their way through the congestion.

and frequently dangerous. The abundance of different forms of coaches—gigs, phaetons, chaises, landaus—added to the traffic tangle.

But this chapter will show throughout that a great spirit of improvement (environmental and otherwise) came into its own in this period—and the roads received their share of it. Some of the improvements were carried out by profit-seekers who had obtained the right to charge a toll for their sections of roads, so that travellers paid, often quite heavily, for rides that were definitely smoother and mostly free from threat of robbery. When the urge for improvement in the Regent's time got into top gear, men like Macadam and Telford were able literally to scrape off the tops of main roads and start afresh. Macadam's surfacing tended to be dusty when dry and muddy when wet, but it was a major advance from the dirt tracks that preceded it.

London Streets

The average London street in the late 18th-century seemed to be a sea of mud, with pedestrians picking their way through filth at the edge, and hordes of wagons and carriages struggling through the centre—always with the risk that people on foot could be struck by an edgy horse, crushed against the houses or simply muddied from head to foot. The better streets were cobbled, which improved the cleanliness but did nothing for the dangers—and added the drawback of appalling noise, thanks to the vehicles' iron-bound wheels. Very few regulations had been devoted to the condition of city streets before 1760: individual householders were in principle responsible for the upkeep of the roadway in front of their doors, but such laws were hardly enforceable. Then in the 1760s came a new set of laws that turned street maintenance over to the municipal corporations, and improvements began. Even the City got busy widening its dark streets, while in Westminster paving stones started to appear, gutters began to be placed at the roadsides, rounded cobbles gave way to flatter stones —all looked after by paid employees of the city. Road-building programmes kept pace: above all the 'New Road' (today the Euston Road that becomes Marylebone Road) was transformed from a dirt track through northern suburbs into a major thoroughfare from Islington towards Paddington, and the acknowledged northern boundary of the main body of London. New roads branched southwards towards Lambeth, others formed a brave network in the west of the city. And by the Regency period there were four new bridges across the Thames as well as London and Westminster bridges: Blackfriars, Vauxhall, Waterloo and Southwark, the last three built between 1813 and 1819. Then, too, the canal-building that had been so useful in the new industrial areas of England also came to London: the Grand Junction canal was cut from London to Warwickshire by 1805, and in later years the Regent's Canal was to be embraced in Nash's spectacular rebuilding scheme for the West End. The canal companies had only a little time to enjoy their success, for the mighty age of railways was into its stride by the 1830s.

Other novelties transformed London streets in the late 18th and early 19th centuries. The 18th-century sedan chair began to vanish as the hackney coach, plying for hire, came into being—making the traffic worse until street improvements caught up with it. Sometimes Londoners who had had to leap for safety to avoid a clattering 'hack' turned in enraged groups to overturn and smash the coach; but such incidents occurred mainly when the hackney was still new. By 1771 there were a thousand hacks on the streets, and people had got used to them. Then in the early 19th century J. A. Hansom invented his cab, with one horse and two wheels, which —though it carried fewer passengers than the six that fitted into the hackney—was compact enough to allow a

...ers
...might
...the line

...l-gate, one of the three new bridges built
...which contributed to the general improve-
...ommunications.

little more room at the edges of narrow streets. Horse-drawn omnibuses also made their appearance in this period: the first ran between the Bank and Paddington (for a fare of 1s.) in 1829, and seven years later there were 400 on the streets. The typical omnibus carried about twenty people in its ungainly oversized coach body, pulled by three or four horses.

While the local authorities were making provision for street widening, paving and the like, they imposed a few extra regulations that, for instance, greatly extended street lighting (far beyond the standard of European cities). Most better-class streets had some form of sewer beneath its pavement—usually a primitive tube of brick, but occasionally iron in later years; and house drains began to improve. So the streets slowly became cleaner and dryer, assisted too by new laws attacking 'nuisances' (householders throwing rubbish and worse into the street and leaving it there, or people digging holes and leaving them with no warning for pedestrians, or herders driving cattle or fowl through paved streets, and much more). Other regulations swept away the individualistic jungle of shop signs, which had come in all sizes, shapes and positions, often stretching completely across the road—and thereby let a great deal more air and light into the city's crowded streets.

The Rich and the Poor

As throughout English history, the Regency was a time when both wealth and poverty existed at almost unimaginable extremes. Isolated figures say comparatively little, but some indication of levels may be gained from the middle ranges: the substantial merchants and many facturers who were doing well at £700 a year; t' smaller shopkeepers maintaining themselves adequa' on £150, and publicans at £100. Top grades of tea: (including university dons) and leading artisans be just above the poverty line at £60 a year, fo

34

was drawn (in 1814) at about £50. But in the reign of George IV skilled workers and craftsmen could reach a more comfortable, nearly middle-class level. Unskilled labourers in towns or out of them fell below the line. Bankers and extremely successful merchants might aspire to about £2,500, and be among the wealthy classes; yet great noblemen might measure the income from their immense estates in the tens or even hundreds of thousands. Far, far below were the unemployed, the petty criminals and vagabonds, fortunate to scrape together even £5 over twelve months.

We tend, because of historical bias, to think of the Regency period in terms of its 'high society'—but these glittering heights were occupied by the wealthy, leisured minority, their numbers swollen slightly by the addition of a few leading politicians, a few of the nouveau-riche industrialists and a scattering of fashionable artists. These luminaries, fluttering at varying distances from the court and the focuses of power, had little to do with the broad mainstream of London life—which to some extent justified Napoleon's perhaps apocryphal quip about English shopkeepers. The salt of London's earth and the bulk of its population was indeed shopkeepers, along with the various grades of craftsmen, artisans, labourers skilled and semi-skilled. The professions, too, were numerous (and were undergoing upheavals as the age began demanding—and to some extent getting—higher standards of training and competence). In this period professional men rose out of the ranks of superior tradesmen and formed a special class of their own. The period was one of struggles and attempts at clarification and reform within the law, and lawyers proliferated in the Inns of Court. Doctoring seemed to be a profession bestowing a fair amount of social status and a comfortable living, especially if one aspired beyond the role of apothecary (who until 1815 was mostly a tradesman, mixing and dispensing medicines, though perhaps doing a

A *Regency dandy. Note his tightly waisted swallow-tail coat and high, constricting stock.*

little unofficial doctoring among the poor) to the position of surgeon—demanding study, hospital training and some years of application, allowing the successful actually to practise medicine in all its ramifications. Parsons and university dons had their share of status, but they may not have increased too rapidly in numbers, since the remuneration did not always match the social benefits.

The working classes of London seemed in this period to be involved with rather more familiar, traditional occupations than the idea of the industrial revolution would suggest. One historian has pointed out, for instance, that in 1837 there were more woman servants than there were woman millhands in the cotton areas. London industry (apart from the brickworks and the like that fed the booming building trade, and apart from the vast breweries and other exceptions) focused itself on the wide-ranging activity of a great seaport. Ship-building was vital, as was the transport industry generally, concerned with the widespread movement of goods within a great manufacturing and trading nation. Otherwise, London as a producer was a city of high-quality craftsmen, individually occupied (with their apprentices and journeymen) in turning out special goods such as cutlery, clocks, jewellery and furniture. And it was a city of middle-range artisans, above all the superabundant tailors, bootmakers, and building specialists like masons, carpenters and painters. These individuals could claim the higher reaches of status among the working classes; they undoubtedly termed themselves at least as worthy as the most respectable small shopkeepers. Many of them were themselves shopkeepers, as with jewellers or cabinet-makers. On lower rungs were the hordes of clerks, shop-assistants (who were always men) and street-market people (often women). Still lower were the hard-working poor, including unskilled labourers such as porters or stable hands, and the apprentices. This group also includes the hundreds of wandering street pedlars, offering every imaginable sort of ware to passers-by and at house doors, adding more than their share to the enormous din of the city.

Most of this chapter will be looking at Londoners in the middle range and above, sketching in many aspects just how they lived. But space should first be given to how the very poor lived, at the depths, when they succeeded in living at all. They made their homes in the dank warrens of lanes and alleys in the east and southeast, lined with crumbling tenements and appallingly filthy open ditches, and in the mazes of back streets on the fringes of the central area. They lived family by family in small, dark single rooms—garrets or cellars for the most part, while the worst off lived in the streets, or in vacant tumbledown houses. (Some entrepreneurs among the poorer classes made a little money by finding such ruined houses, taking them over, and charging 2d. a night to the homeless.) Of course the artisan and the fully employed labourer also lived with his family in a single room, for on this level London's housing problem was as great as at any time since. It was the quality of the room, the house, the furniture if any, that made the distinction. Among the great mass of unemployed, the one bed that held the entire family might be nothing more than a pile of stinking rags; and it might constitute the only 'furniture' in the room. These bottom-of-the-scale people wore rags, or near-rags, as well as sleeping on them; their food when they had any would strike us as unfit for human consumption; and they earned the pennies necessary to stay alive by casual labour (perhaps on the wharves, or carrying loads in the market), or by begging, or especially by all forms of petty and not-so-petty crime.

Of course, there was an alternative—for some provision had been made in British law towards the relief of the poor. It consisted mainly of poorhouses for the old and infirm and workhouses, or state-operated work programmes, to occupy and feed the able-bodied. In theory each parish looked after its own, supported by the rates. In practice, the programme was corrupt, slipshod and ineffective—though to be sure it was not helped by the traditional unwillingness of the Englishman, however badly off, to give up his independence. Nor was it helped by the typical fear of the authorities that if the workhouses were made too attractive they would encourage indigence among the working classes. In fact, they bent over backwards to make the relief of the poor wholly unpleasant, adding extra strength to the pauper's determination to stay out whenever possible, whatever his straits. For that matter, until the Poor Laws were reorganised in the early 19th century, the scarcity of available workhouses also kept many of the needy out. (That Poor Law reform also did away with the state subsidies existing in some areas, aimed to fill out the wages of the employed—a worthy welfare theory, but leading in fact to serious inconsistencies, and to prevention of any useful rises in wage scales.)

Naturally, the worst sufferings occurred among the children of the poor—those who survived. The reasonably lucky ones were those taken on by artisans or tradesmen as apprentices, which could be rewarding if the master was a craftsman who would teach the boy a valuable skill. But more often the masters merely sought boys as the cheapest available labour to carry on their business. Apprentices received board, lodging and clothing (on which the master spent no more than he had to), worked long hours (16 hours a day was a usual average), were bound to the master generally for seven years, and were totally subject to him whatever the nature of the treatment. The worst off were the parish apprentices, who were virtually sold to the employers, and who were taught little or nothing. They would mostly be orphans, foundlings or illegitimates, or the children of poorhouse

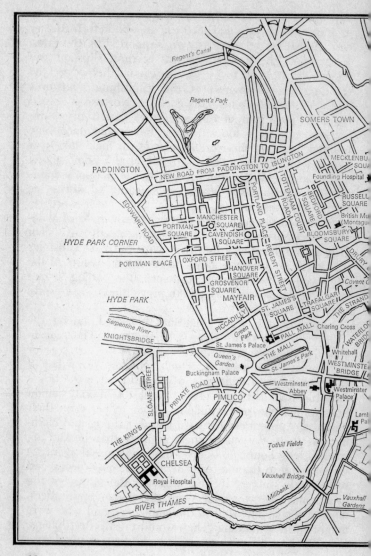

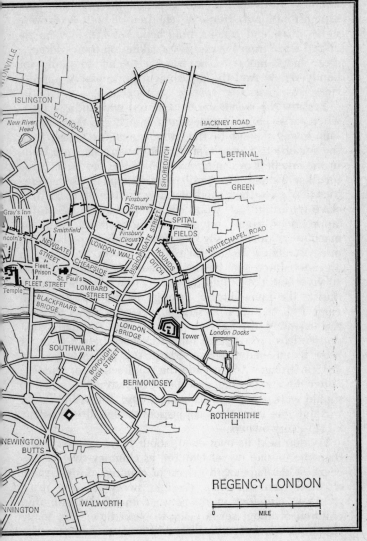

REGENCY LONDON

0   MILE   1

families. Ill-treatment was commonplace, murder and rape astonishingly frequent (children of both sexes were indentured) and seldom punished. Yet the masters received a fee from the parish for taking on the children, a clear inducement to the worst elements to apply for handy slaves. And the punishment for runaway apprentices was invariably speedy and severe.

Perhaps the worst abuses occurred with industrialism, when parish children were sent in bunches to the northern mill towns, bound to the mill-owners for years (from the age of 8 to 21 was typical), set to work far from home in the cruellest of conditions—with little provision made for their welfare, and hardly any attempt by the authorities to oversee their condition. It was little different from slave trade: in fact, if the employer's factory failed, the 'apprentices' could be sold outright along with the machinery. More usually they were simply turned out: in one instance, a cartload of child labourers was taken to an uninhabited spot by the sea and simply unloaded, to survive how they could, or not. A few reforms came in during the humanitarian upsurge in the late 18th and early 19th centuries, and their provisions serve to show the extent of the horror: one new law stipulated that apprentices must not be forced to work before 6 am or after 9 pm, and this was considered philanthropic. In 1815 a stronger Act forbade the employment of children under the age of nine, and stated that no child under 16 should work more than 12 hours a day. (But enforcement was dubious, since the local justices tended also to be the local factory owners.)

London held its own child-labour horrors, none worse than the unique use of children as chimney-sweeps. Because of the haphazard nature of chimney design, small children were the only possible sweepers: the usual chimney, one foot in diameter, demanded small, thin children of about seven years to clean them. But many chimneys were even smaller, and four- or five-year-olds were sent into them—usually naked so their clothing would not cause them to be jammed. Often a child would be sent into a chimney that was on fire, to put out the flames; always the children were injured by scraping against the chimney's sides, or by falling—or, indeed, by the cruelty of their master, who may well have taken on the children as 'apprentices' but may equally well have stolen them. Again the reforms of this practice (in 1788) reveal its nature, for the new laws forbade children under eight being taken into the trade, forbade sending them into burning chimneys, and ordered that they be washed once a *week*. In the early 1800s, when a sweeping machine had been invented, the 'climbing boys' were supposed to be no more; but aristocratic homes still had small chimney flues (even in newly built homes a seven-inch flue was common), and the practice continued well into the 19th century.

Disease and Sanitation

What passes for statistics about the 18th century shows that, before George III, London burials exceeded in number London baptisms. Not that this fact meant a decrease in population, as many optimists then believed —for a great percentage of the burials must have been infants dying before baptism, and the steadily increasing influx of immigrants—especially the Irish, who formed a large portion of the miserably poor of the city—kept the overall number of Londoners on the rise. After 1760, however, baptisms caught up with and surpassed burials —except for comparatively brief periods when times were hard (as when harvests failed for some years in the 1790s) or when epidemics of disease swept through the crowded slums. And also excepting the probable thousands of deaths in the period that were never entered in the official registers. But in spite of these qualifications, it seems proved that the lot of the common man did improve enormously in late Georgian times, even if standards of living still seem shocking compared even to those of the later 19th century. If nothing else, the London masses had an improved chance of staying alive. And much of the decline in the mortality rate grew out of a noticeable decline in disease—thanks to developments in sanitation and medicine.

The greater cleanliness and dryness of London's streets has been mentioned. Hand in hand with these advances went innovations within the house. Water, for instance, which had always been brought to household cisterns by wagons, or fetched by servants from the parish pump, now began to come by pipes—even though the pipes were often merely wood, or sometimes lead. Roof gutters and run-off pipes by then were obligatory in most parts of London; and these plumbing developments led to a variety of experimentation with water closets, to replace the foul 'privies' that were normal additions to every back garden. Most of the early versions made little provision against separating the pan of the w.c. from the cesspool or drain, and when traps were invented to cut off the stench they were seldom self-cleansing. Neither these advances—nor the fact that the newly piped water-supply came straight from the foetid Thames—may seem to deserve the name of sanitation. But they show progress, at least of intention, from the earlier days when water came from any nearby source, however befouled, or when refuse and human waste were simply tossed into the street or into a nearby open ditch. Even so, it was to take considerably more time to rid the city of similarly filthy practices—such as that of slaughtering animals in open markets (or even in private houses) and throwing the offal into the ditch or roadway; or of burying paupers in gruesome mass graves, great open pits that were not *covered* until they were completely full, and were not full until they each held about 20 or 25 bodies.

Disease enough, it is clear, could spread from this

general foulness of London air, water and the very earth. But without doubt the epidemics were growing less frequent, and fatal to relatively fewer people, than in the mid-18th century. Typhus, and various illnesses vaguely classified as 'fevers', were perhaps the most common killers at that time, but their incidence declined dramatically after 1770. Smallpox appeared briefly to increase, but mainly because early forms of immunisation turned the immunised temporarily into carriers. When vaccination came along after the 1790s, another major cause of death began to decline. Other widespread diseases were at least contained, if not defeated, by advances in medical practice, which must be among the finer accomplishments of the Regency urge to improvement. The first experiments with anaesthesia took place in the early 19th century, looking forward to the time when no more full-scale surgical operations would have to be conducted on fully conscious, screaming patients. Other advances in medicine included the demand in 1815 that apothecaries must undergo a period of formal training and sit an examination—whereas before they had merely to go through some years as an apprentice to an apothecary, learning perhaps little or nothing.

Hospitals improved as well, even in those days before antiseptic when injuries, operations, childbirth and so on led to a terrible death rate from infection. Small dispensaries devoted to working-class patients did much to propagandise the value of sanitation, fresh air and cleanliness, and apparently had a better average of cures than the great hospitals (where in the 1770s St. Bartholomew's averaged a death every 13 patients and considered that rate an improvement). Even then, long before Pasteur, some observant dispensary doctors saved lives by the use of isolation to counter contagious diseases. With this, and the new tendency to cleanse (with hot lime) houses where the infection of 'fever' had been found, the annual deaths from fever were halved from 1801 to 1815. And

A Cruikshank cartoon pillorying venal doctors who deliberately promote disease. In fact, improved medicine had enormously reduced the number and virulence of epidemics.

like-minded doctors were beginning to eradicate one of the great killers of the time, 'child-bed (puerperal) fever', by the simple process of keeping the hospital, the beds, the mothers and themselves as clean as possible.

Eating Habits

The foregoing advances in preventative medicine were helped, in their assault on disease, by a general raising of dietary standards in late Georgian times. The 18th-century defeat of scurvy had been a lesson to everyone: by the end of the century, fresh vegetables were being taken for granted as near-necessities in the capital, as market gardens proliferated outside the city. But then eating habits generally were changing (though not always for the better, as instanced by the growing craze for white bread in fashionable London that led shady bakers to whiten the flour with chalk or white ash).

The general improvement of living standards among employed workers and upwards meant that newer foods were appearing on their menus. Wider varieties of fish came in as transport from fishing areas speeded up; the 'made dishes' of foreign climes—ragouts, fricassees, and so on—gained in popularity as trade and war and immigration made London more cosmopolitan. The old prejudice against fresh fruit, as being 'indigestible', had virtually died out. But still the great traditions of English cooking persisted in all their strength: meat remained the centrepiece of most meals, and lots of it—roast or boiled mainly, with beef and mutton the predominant favourites. Bacon was another mainstay of the working people, veal was popular among the well-off. Dinners were enormous, moving through an abundant fish course (say, fried smelts, or salmon with fennel sauce and butter) to the main dishes that might burden the table with chickens, ham, a giant roast, and varieties of meat pies (pigeon was a favourite) rich with eggs. Plum pudding, gooseberry or currant tarts might top off the meal—with plenty of nuts or assorted fruits for after-dinner nibbling. Invariably the food was rich and heavy (except among the more fastidious members of the upper ranks): one of the mighty meat pies could have six pounds of butter in the pastry, while a popular sweet called a 'hedgehog' demanded six eggs, a quart of almonds and a quart of cream.

The traditions of heaviness and abundance also persisted in English drinking habits. The working classes and most of the middle classes washed down their bread and cheese or their roast meat with quantities of beer

47

and stout. The poor had to make do with 'small beer', a considerably less potent beverage. The better-off preferred wines—port, sherry, 'sack' were always popular—or else abandoned alcohol and drank coffee and chocolate, and the still comparatively recent innovation of tea. (The latter suffered quite a few price rises throughout the 18th century, and was also considered by many people, even in Regency times, to be unhealthy.)

London Crime

In the middle of the 18th century, any close looks at poverty, at illness and at table habits in London all seemed to focus on the terrifying problem of cheap gin—so cheap that it could be the solace of even the most miserably poor, but also their eventual killer. Gin had been both an escape from a life of misery and a cause and effect of a high crime rate in the 1750s, as the poorer classes turned to crime when drunk or in order to get drunk. Eventually strong government measures came in—after an immense struggle with the distillers' pressure group—to control the production and the price of gin. The crime rate began to fall—though it underwent a spurt after the end of the war, when thousands of unemployed veterans suddenly clogged the cities. And it would have a long way to fall before it could be said to be under control.

Theft of all kinds, understandably, dominated the crime rolls—from petty pilfering through burglary to large and organised gangs of thieves and pickpockets. (But early versions of equally organised police forces, such as the predecessors of the famous 'Bow Street Runners', had by Regency times broken up most of the worst gangs of street robbers.) Crimes of violence were everyday affairs, often accompanying robbery; and the poorer districts of London could always be positively dangerous for a well-dressed man after dark. Yet, again, the general

A *highwayman robbing a wealthy traveller. The menace of high-way robbers and 'footpads' diminished as roads were improved and better patrolled in the late 18th century.*

improvements of living conditions discouraged the spread of such areas, and so partially contained crime: improved roads and means of transport (and the guarded toll roads) reduced the number of highwaymen and 'footpads' that previously infested the fringes of the city; while improved streets and lighting within the city had their effect on townsmen. But it seems that the widespread crimes of confidence, trickery, fraud, embezzlement, forgery and the like were less easily remedied— then as now. Certainly counterfeiting was an important crime in those days before money contained built-in safeguards. Prostitution appears not to have been a crime, but vagrancy was—and any homeless and penniless pauper outside the workhouse was by definition a vagrant. In fact, in a way poverty was a crime, since men could still be imprisoned for debt well into the 19th century.

The criminal law in general remained fairly barbarous until that century, when a few long overdue reforms came in that give a clear picture of crime and punishment previously. The reforms were spearheaded by Sir Robert Peel, Home Secretary and later Prime Minister; he managed to sweep several absurd and outdated laws off the books (such as that which imposed the death penalty for damaging Westminster Bridge). By 1832 death was no longer the punishment for stealing horses or sheep, or for housebreaking. After 1838 murder and attempted murder were the only remaining crimes for which hanging was the punishment. And as for debtors, the reforms managed after years of struggle to do away with the law that imprisoned men for owing less than £20, though it was not until 1869 that imprisonment for larger debts was abolished.

The forerunners of an organised police force have been mentioned; but the early nucleus of officers that later became the Bow Street Runners were more comparable to our detectives than to uniformed constables, and were few. Regency parishes had their handfuls of constables, appointed by local justices of the peace, and presumably some were more or less honest and devoted to their jobs. Apart from them, there were the 'thief-takers'—we might call them 'bounty-hunters'—working for rewards; there were unofficial watchmen hired by men with something to lose, like the warehouse owners at the docks; and there were the generally inefficient and often corrupt 'Charlies', the city watch that in practice did little more than call out the hours, and that not always accurately. Magistrates there were in plenty, mostly unpaid and so wide open to bribery. Eventually Peel began to press for a more organised opposition to the world of crime; and one or two rumbustious riots around 1820 convinced the government that it was indeed time the London mob had some control imposed upon it. An Act drawn up by Peel established the Metropolitan Police (at Scotland Yard) in 1829.

Entertainments

It is sometimes difficult to draw a clear line between the crimes of 18th-century Londoners and their amusements, in whatever class. Leisure time at both the top and the bottom of society seemed to be given over to drinking and gambling, both great breeding-grounds of crime. The rougher elements maintained some of their traditional enjoyments, most of which were violent and cruel (perhaps reflecting the violence and cruelty of life as these men saw it): bull-baiting, dog-fights, cockfights and the like. A law passed in 1822 to stop these pastimes had little immediate effect, but other laws in 1833 and 1835 finally clamped down on bull-baiting, at least. (The gradual disappearance of the other cruelties to animals was also accomplished in the 19th century, assisted no doubt by the formation of the RSPCA in 1824.)

But though these ugly occasions for gambling and

riotous enjoyment diminished, others stayed very much alive. Well-off men, especially the wilder young ones, found London night-life richly exciting. Clubs had become a feature of the city in the mid-18th century, and continued to be so, most especially the more raffish drinking and gaming clubs, some of them regular meeting places for particular groups of young bloods and whatever women they could gather, others more public—and more crowded, more wild, more violent. There were, too, somewhat quieter tavern clubs, having something in common with our century's 'working men's clubs', where members might gather for a few drinks, some songs, gossip and a game of dominoes. But other versions of these meeting places could hardly be distinguishable from the unruly clubs (often in taverns) where drunkenness and heavy gambling were the rule. The upper classes had their clubs as well—Brooks's and Crockford's were among the more famous—where gaming went on as extensively as anywhere, but where manners were more controlled and other activities more decorous (and where the intrusion of women was rare). Some of London's best-known modern clubs began after 1815, including the Travellers', the Athenaeum and the Garrick.

Theatres showed less variety than clubs, because the Lord Chamberlain restricted the number of officially licensed theatres to three—Covent Garden, Drury Lane and the Haymarket opera house. These were respectable, but their productions did little good to the standards of 18th-century drama. The unlicensed theatres that popped up here and there were not respectable, but did no more for the drama. Moralists of the time attacked them for attracting disorderly elements—prostitutes looking for customers, entrepreneurs selling drink at high prices, thieves and pickpockets. Other attacks were aimed at plays of dubious morality—though lewdness was probably less common than mere rudeness. After 1832 the city began to pay less attention to the 'illegality' of the

A cross-section of a London audience in 1836. In the pit are the respectable middle-class; in the boxes, those aspiring to fashion; and in the gallery, the rougher element.

unlicensed theatres, and the standards of the theatre improved along with its status—though it still remained proverbial among theatre managers that extravagant spectaculars and lowbrow comedies spelled the fullest houses.

Fashionable society and the upper classes could occupy their leisure, if they wished to, with organised amusements from morning to night. (Of course, some members of this group, such as the political lords or the landowners, spent a good deal of their time actually at work.) The 18th-century habit of morning parties called 'levees' died out slowly in London circles; going calling at fashionable houses at breakfast or before was commonplace. The 18th-century craze for gambling carried into all the best drawing rooms, where the days might be spent at hazard or faro, whist or quinze. Dancing frequently occupied the evenings—at least during the London 'season', when the nobility were in their town houses. The minuet and similar stately, formalised dances maintained their popularity, but by the Regency times more intimate foreign forms such as the waltz—wherein the partners actually embraced—had begun to shock older members of high society. Though most of the important dances or balls were held in private homes, there were high-toned public places like Almack's (begun in 1765) where for a subscription of 10 guineas the top people could attend weekly balls and acquire notable social distinction. But of course the most glittering occasions were Court functions, as epitomised by the great fête staged by the Regent in 1811, where the resplendent decorations included an artificial miniature canal and fountain, complete with fishes, and where the 3000 guests included high European royalty.

The Regency period was a sporting time as well, and it seems that horse racing (stimulated by the gambling fever) had the greatest following. Interest in the races declined a little in wartime, but picked up again after

54

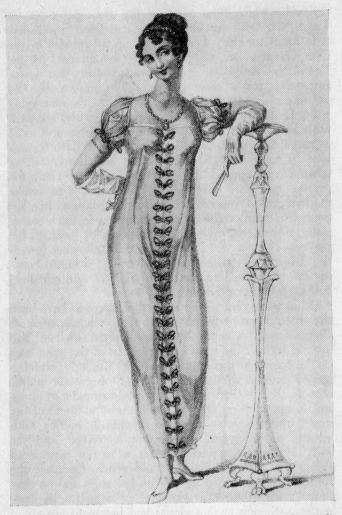

A French Empire ball dress (about 1809) in a comparatively simple
and loosely flowing style when contrasted to earlier restricting and
extravagant ladies' fashions.

1815—by which time many of the great flat races (St Leger, the Oaks and the Derby) had been established. The Ascot tradition was building up at the end of the 18th century, and steeplechasing (though not yet the Grand National) drew great crowds. Betting was heavy, but some effort at control of fraud and other abuses did not materialise till Victorian days—though handicapping came in earlier. As for other spectator sports, armchair athletes and gamblers alike were being more and more attracted to cricket, the rules of which had been formalised in early Georgian times. The first Lord's cricket ground was opened (by Thomas Lord) in 1787, the present one after 1814. The game seems most unlike modern cricket: no standardised dress (players often appeared in wildly coloured shirts, umpires in frock coats); noisy crowds, rowdy betting, no gloves or pads on the players. The bat was light and curved, allowing few of the delicate precision strokes seen today; overarm bowling did not come into practice until 1830, and remained suspect for years afterwards.

Other team games such as football seem to have been the special property of upper-class schools such as Charterhouse. Though townsmen might kick a ball around for fun, the formal organisation of the game as a public spectacle was long in coming. Similarly, athletics stayed mostly within the precincts of certain public schools, though there might be the odd running or jumping competition on open fields in the city. Some of the more brutal sports—bare-fisted fighting, battles with swords or quarter-staffs, wrestling—survived into the early 19th century, but by then were not considered things that a decent person could watch. Certainly the forms of boxing known then, with few rules and no time limits, makes the modern version seem puerile by comparison—though boxing gloves had begun to appear in George IV's time.

The rich continued to engage in the traditional country

amusements of hunting (already taking on most of its present overtones of privilege and snobbery) and shooting, which was extended by improved firearms becoming available. In the city, however, the fashionable set restricted their outdoor diversions to riding (carriages or horseback) or strolling in the parks, primarily in St. James's or Regent's Park when it was completed—or in some of the less crowded public gardens. The ordinary folk also rushed into parks in their leisure hours, or went out to the environs of the city for a stroll on Hampstead Heath, in Epping Forest and other open lands. Numerous pleasure gardens offered enjoyment (if not always peaceful, thanks to the crowds): Londoners flocked to the Vauxhall gardens, and to Ranelagh, Marylebone and elsewhere, to pay a few pence for tea and a snack, to walk among trees and flowers, and on special evenings to listen to concerts or be thrilled by firework displays. Outside the city, in ex-urban villages like Highbury or Hornsey, smaller tea gardens were popular and refreshments cheaper; many Londoners also patronised gardens associated with mineral springs (or 'spas') such as the Hampstead Spa (at Well Walk) or the more fashionable Sadler's Wells. At the latter, besides open-air entertainment and medicinal waters, was the increasingly famous playhouse that offered a wide variety of entertainment, from acrobatics to ballet.

Of course the masses of Londoners had less variety in their amusement generally than the upper classes, for they worked all week and then faced the dismal prospect of a circumscribed Sunday. In theory at least such activities as riding or travelling for recreation, sports and games, and of course any form of commerce was forbidden by law on the Lord's Day. But by the early 1800s the people had begun to ignore this inhibiting regulation, and though churchmen deplored the shattering of the Sabbath by shopkeepers and street pedlars, sportsmen and pleasure seekers, reformers would point out that if

Vauxhall Gardens (about 1800). Pleasure Gardens continued to attract all classes in Regency times.

certain amusements were not allowed on the Londoner's one day of leisure he would spend it entirely in taverns and public houses. (Oddly, the same churchmen who complained about men playing cricket on Sunday almost never objected to men sitting soddenly in public houses on that day.)

Of all London's opportunities for amusement, the great fairs take pride of place. Among them were such traditional festivities as Bartholomew's Fair, originating in medieval times and at its peak in the 17th century but still highly popular among the 'mob' in the 18th, offering an immense range of shows, entertainers, and refreshment. The lower classes also still patronised such older fairs as the May Fair in Shepherd's Market, with its versions of theatrical entertainment, contests and sideshows—or Tottenham Fair, outside the city but near enough to draw crowds. Frost fairs, held in winter if the Thames froze over, were still known in the late 18th century, with showmen performing on the ice, taverns hastily erected, and the special joy of crossing the river on foot without a bridge. Greenwich had a great fair as well as a park and tea gardens; and many of the large marketplaces, like Covent Garden or Smithfields, had a 'fringe' of refreshment stalls and the like that lent them the atmosphere of fairs. And the main festive seasons of Whitsun, Easter and Christmas (the only times when Londoners experienced anything resembling a public holiday) were always celebrated by a host of small fairs springing up in gardens and fields throughout the city.

Regency Fashions

Fashion in clothing has always been changeable, by very virtue of the name. But many of the changes in Regency times were semi-permanent and far-reaching, ushering in trends that have continued until today. Among the most striking and important innovations was the sudden availability, thanks to the booming textile industry, of inexpensive cotton clothing. It gave the poor a better chance of being suitably clothed, but above all it allowed higher standards of cleanliness: no longer were undergarments made from heavy wool, unwashable and so never washed, or corsets and stays made from equally uncleanable leather. Cotton could be washed; in better-off families more changes of clothing became possible; and the result was an extra contribution to the growing fight against disease and infection in the cities.

A few paragraphs cannot hope to do justice to the fantastic alterations in feminine fashion during the period. Let it suffice that one most unusual extreme of ladies' dress occurred during the heyday of the Regency. Dresses had long been becoming less formal, and some authorities credit the rise of Romanticism with the freeing of ladies from their extravagant gowns, towering headdresses, encumbering petticoats and crippling stays. Certainly freedom became the watchword, for at the height of the fad a fashionable lady might well attend a ball wearing a very simply cut dress, on vaguely classical lines, clinging to the body, exceptionally décolleté—and little else. Not only corsets but petticoats were abandoned: 'like Mother Eve our maids may stray ashamed,' commented Lord Byron without too much exaggeration. Sadly, the fashion soon gave way to more demure garb, which preceded the voluminous skirts and plethora of petticoats of Victorianism. Corsets were worn again, as the waistline of dresses descended from its former position only slightly below the breasts, and as fashion began to dictate its extreme tininess. But one sweeping change remained: instead of the simple shift that in the 18th century constituted a lady's most basic undergarment (and in which she usually slept as well), the Regency women had begun wearing knickers. At the same time the idea of a special flimsy gown for bed-wear had caught on, and never died out.

Beau Brummell, an enormously influential leader of fashion; he introduced the wearing of trousers at the beginning of the 19th century.

In those days men's fashions changed as often and as radically as women's; professional men of fashion spent fortunes on keeping up with (or ahead of) the leading 'Beau' of the time. None was more memorable than the Regent's friend (for a while) Beau Brummell, whose influence on dress was so great that he alone was able to create and popularise the fashion of trousers. (It must have brought him many praises from the men whose calves were too fat or thin to look well in the tight silk stockings that went with 18th-century breeches.) Pictures of Regency men reveal them in the most elegantly cut swallow-tail coats, nipped in tightly at the waist; and the relative comfort of their trousers was countered by the strangulation of very high 'stocks'—wide cravats wound several times around the neck. At least the spirit of freedom as displayed by the ladies was echoed in the men by the gradual disappearance of the powdered white wigs of the 18th century; though some professions (including doctors and footmen) retained them well into the 19th, and lawyers have not quite given them up even yet.

The less fashionable folk of London allowed their clothing to change very little over the years, and hardly at all at the dictates of fads. Shopkeepers would be seen in respectable dark-coloured coats of wool or velvet, quiet waistcoats (perhaps silk), breeches, stockings and so on. And this standard 18th-century garb succumbed very slowly to such suspect innovations as trousers. Workmen usually dressed according to their trade (the baker in white, the butcher in blue), and most craftsmen wore aprons of some sort when at work. The poorer classes wore what they could get: one of the indications of the greater prosperity of Regency times was the increase in shoes seen on the feet of working-class Londoners.

Interior Decoration

Wealthy Englishmen in the late Georgian world were as concerned with decorating the insides of their houses as

A tea chest design by Hepplewhite (1789), decorated with a 'classical' motif. Classicism remained the dominant inspiration for designers and architects in Regency times.

with the outsides of their persons. The new prosperity in the reign of George III had given rise to something of a reaction against the fairly ponderous lines of the dominant 'Palladian' school of 18th-century building, and Robert Adam with his flair for ornamentation caught the mood exactly. Rooms by Adam and his contemporaries seemed lighter and more airy than before—free from the Palladian rules, more gay with 'frills' of elegant mouldings and plasterwork, decorated ceilings that might be highly coloured or a more restrained white and gold. Adam's decor, and that of his later imitators, was no less overdone, affected and extravagant than the whole fashionable scene of the time: but it takes an extra helping of dourness to make one ignore or dismiss the unquestioned flair and style of both. (More of Adam's characteristic touches will be seen in later discussions of specific houses.) Some architects, understandably, reacted away from the post-Adam extremes of ornament and decoration, and the cleaner, simpler lines of the later Regency period emerged—except when the Regent himself lavished quantities of money on something like his oriental extravaganza at Brighton. Or except when fashionable romanticism threw up a taste for the Gothic, which created more than its share of monstrosities of building and decor.

Elegance, simplicity and a highly developed sense of proportion define the furniture of the 18th century—with certain exceptions, as when the designers succumbed to the craze for supposedly oriental motifs. (So the 1760s had an abundance of heavy, decorated furniture in lacquer work—and hand-painted Chinese wallpaper had begun to be imported by the very rich.) A good deal of the time's elegance and undeniable beauty came out of a spirit of standardisation: the great 18th-century furniture designers—Chippendale, Hepplewhite, Sheraton—had all published their books by Regency times, and their ideas had filtered down to (and had been adapted by) the smallest back-street cabinet makers. This is partly why it is impossible today to identify, say, a Sheraton chair as being actually of the craftsman's own time or his own design. In the same way, the mass-production methods of Wedgwood and others allowed a wide range of people to have excellent, inexpensive china in their homes. So in the early prosperous times of the late Georgian period, even the ordinary middle-class Londoner could afford a taste of the 'age of elegance'.

Education and the Arts

Something of the change in the arts around the turn of the century has already been briefly described. Two characteristic threads can be isolated (which also appear in architectural and design changes): first, a general sense of release, a freedom from the 'rules' of proportion and propriety imposed by 18th-century classicists, soon outworn and desiccated; second, a movement towards everything that is implied in the then often-used word 'picturesque', which we can find in the poems of Shelley, the landscapes of Constable, the dramatic terraces of

A caricature by Gillray of the Prince Regent. Although unpopular for his self-indulgence, he was, nevertheless, a discerning and influential patron of the arts.

Nash. In a way, it is the spirit of reform and liberalism that can be seen in these trends, altered perhaps but not out of recognition. So it can in the corresponding developments on less heavy levels: the rise of liberal periodicals like the *Examiner* of Leigh Hunt (a minor poet and radical journalist who spent a time in prison for his attacks on the Regent); or the growing importance of individualistic essayists like Hazlitt or Lamb. Equally important were the changes that made British culture accessible to a much wider range of society. For example, in 1770 London held only four circulating libraries; after 1820 there were over 100, and nearly 2000 smaller book clubs. For another example, British art had received a boost from the formation of the Royal Academy in 1768, but received a much greater one— especially from the standpoint of dissemination—when the Regent himself bought a collection of paintings and put up a building to house them, creating the National Gallery. An equally great contribution was made by the Regent when he had become king, and gave the King's library to the nation—requiring a considerable expansion of the British Museum from 1823. The foundation of the Royal Academy of Music in 1823 began the process of reviving interest in British music; the London Philharmonic Society and other smaller musical groups laboured to maintain musical standards and yet to reach wider audiences.

If the culture was expanding in this period, so was education. Reform elements began to believe, as part of their humanitarian progress, in the diffusion of education among the lower classes, and a good number of organisations and institutes—usually charitable and often religious—were set up to infuse at least some rudiments of knowledge, and literacy, into the 'mob'. At the same time, for the middle classes and above, public lectures began to gain tremendous popularity—lectures in the sciences and the arts, of varying standards but at least indicating the educational mood. On a higher level, the narrow monopoly of university education held by Oxford and Cambridge was broken by the establishment of the University of London in 1828. Oxbridge insisted that its entrants be members of the established church; London countered this exclusiveness, for it insisted on no religious education within its walls. Soon the established church struck back with a rival institution in London, King's College in the Strand.

Architecture

This subject has been intentionally left to the last, because—buildings being the only link across time that we have with the Regency period—architecture will crop up extensively in the following chapters. To clarify the late sections, some general sketch of architectural developments during the reigns of George III and IV is appropriate.

Earlier Georgian building had been characterised by a high sense of proportion and decorum, in the Palladian style imported from Italy some time before by Inigo Jones and others. (We can ignore the earliest explorations in Walpole's day into the idea of the Gothic, for those times had little real knowledge of medieval principles and their Gothic constructions deserved the term 'Follies' so often applied to them.) The decorous approach led to enormous changes in the look of London: where previously a variety of styles would be clashingly close-packed along a street, the 18th century saw that the necessity of crowding houses together need not result in haphazard mixtures. So the uniformity of terraces came to the city. Even when Robert Adam and the other Adams began undermining the Palladian ways, they did little to the fronts of houses: any changes in typical Georgian façades were intended to improve the lighting of the rooms, and the general gracefulness of the lines of the building. Uniformity of terraces remained the watchword—as can be seen still in the smooth, plain frontages on, say, Harley Street.

Much of this formal correctness was discarded in the great building boom that occurred in George IV's time—dominated by the more palatial approach of Nash, who imposed movement and variety on his frontages (anathema in earlier years). The terraces were still being built, but so indeed was the reasonably new innovation of semi-detached houses (by which two middle-class houses could together partake of the move towards 'grandeur' that had become fashionable). The novelties in the columns and porticos of Nash's time were paralleled by, among other things, the introduction of stucco—intended to give a building the appearance of masonry—instead of the red or brown brick of Georgian buildings.

Two more changes in British architecture should be mentioned. One has already been hinted at: that the period reached new heights of building and design because of its stretches of prosperity, which encouraged men (usually the landowning nobility) to speculate by the construction of important estates in and near London—interconnected and uniformly designed buildings focused on a square, or developments of major streets or larger areas. The first great building boom occurred in the newly rich days of George III; the second began when the post-war recession had been overcome, after 1820. And the building booms were accompanied by a far-reaching change among the builders themselves. In early Georgian times construction was overseen by a master-builder, correlating and organising the work of the various craftsmen—masons, carpenters, and so on—from whose ranks he might have risen. Or building designs were obtained from practical men like surveyors, or more or less knowledgeable amateurs among the gentry. But in the Regency period architecture became a profession. It acquired recognised, practical standards; it acquired professional status and respectability; it demanded knowledge, above all, of the accessible styles of other places and times and of current needs and fashions. When in 1791 a group of London architects formed a dining club, the profession had certainly arrived; it consolidated its arrival by its incorporation as the Royal Institute of British Architects in 1837. By then the training of architects (mostly in the offices of the established professionals) and their practice had become formalised, authoritative and fully in control of the progress of British building.

The Spreading City

The late Georgian era must have been a builder's para-
dise, not simply because of the continuing and inevitable
growth of the city, but because that period saw two of
the largest building booms in London's history till then.
The growth and general expansion moved in a great
many directions from the radial hub of the City; but the
building booms, when the leading architects, estate
owners and speculators, were concentrating their efforts,
took place principally to the west and north. Slowly the
City's role as the hub began its decline: slowly the
fashionable heart of the capital, the cynosure of Londoners, moved west. It could be found in what we now
call Bloomsbury and Holborn during the early 18th century, and the importance of that area lasted well into the
Regency.

Gray's Inn Road, Bloomsbury's eastern boundary, had
been a fashionable promenade as well as a key coach
route into London (Fielding's Tom Jones entered the city
that way). But by the later years of the century the
movement away from the area led to a decline, and

where leading merchants had had their shops were now some of the worst taverns, gambling dens and brothels of George III's day—as well as a major quarter for Irish immigrants whose incredible poverty made native English paupers seem well off. The Royal Free Hospital was established in the early 19th century in this area to give free treatment to the 'destitute sick', which underlines the district's fall as much as it does the increasing rise of humanitarianism.

In 18th-century Bloomsbury, the present main thoroughfare of Southampton Row was a quiet back street ending at High Holborn; in 1760 it afforded the poet Thomas Gray an uninterrupted view of fields stretching northwards to Hampstead. Gower Street, the other major north-south artery of Bloomsbury, was also a quiet residential street built up in Regency times; but it blossomed as a scholarly centre after the King's Library had been moved into the remodelled British Museum, and more so when University College rose on the street as the nucleus of the country's third university. Tottenham Court Road, the western boundary of the district, had a much greater importance in the 18th century—not only as a main road, but as a centre for some of the more wide-open amusements of the time. The southern end of that road shaded into the rat-warren of tenements at St. Giles called the 'Rookery'; the northern end, at the New Road (Euston Road), held a lively pleasure garden. From there the pioneer balloonist Lunardi ascended in 1785: and there a giant fair was held annually until early 19th-century builders moved in to develop the site.

Within Bloomsbury, the focus is of course Bloomsbury Square, said to be the first of the estate developments to bear the name of a square. In late Georgian times the lordly house that dominated that square was pulled down, and terraces were built across its northern side as part of the immense development of the Bedford Estate —which included Bedford Square farther west, Russell and Tavistock squares northwards, and many more. Great Russell Street was the heart-line of the area, and had been since the 17th century when the Earl of Southampton first made Bloomsbury into a desirable suburb. There are still a few pleasant, unpretentious late Georgian houses along this street, but much of its character was wrecked when the Regency demolition crews got busy making room for the expanding British Museum. Deeper into Bloomsbury, off Guilford Street (once a central road of the Foundling Hospital Estate that was begun in the late 18th century), are lesser roads and squares that have retained much of their Georgian aspect—even if some eyes see them, as did one 19th-century writer, as so many 'brick walls with holes in them'. Certainly the plain frontages and street-long uniformity of, say, a Doughty Street, might well call up such a description—if one happened to be an admirer of Victorian Gothic excrescences.

South of Bloomsbury (which means south of New Oxford Street and High Holborn) was one of the liveliest and most populous areas of the mid-18th century and after—the stamping ground of Dr Johnson, among others. Part of this area, though, was cluttered (towards Soho) by the terrible filth, poverty and crime of the Rookery, which remained until irate Londoners forced the authorities to begin, in the 1840s, one of the city's first slum clearance programmes. But the more civilised sections of this south Holborn area held many of the key points of Georgian London: Lincoln's Inn, a most prominent professional man's residential area well into and past the Regency; that legal preserve the Temple; Fleet Street and the Strand, and Covent Garden. And it contains, or contained, two of the most notable structures of George III's reign: Somerset House, still extant, and the Adelphi, now long gone.

Somerset House was built (1776–80) by a leading architect of the time, Sir William Chambers, who brought an air of restraint or even conservatism into an otherwise lively architectural time. The construction filled a need for a grand public building to contain an array of civil servants and services; and grand it was—with its great central courtyard, its flowing arches and Doric columns, and its perhaps superabundance of decorative sculpture. But the modern build-up of the Strand has done little to enhance it. The Somerset House complex now seems too awkwardly placed to be properly impressive. Yet it (and those portions of its original interiors that remain) still offer a worthy example of the more decorous and controlled architecture of the period—considerably less flamboyant, but also less insistently attractive, than the Adam style which was then in its heyday.

The Adam brothers erected their brilliant Adelphi before Chambers set to work on Somerset House, and by rights it should have been the high point of the building boom that characterised the newly rich, heady world of the 1760s. It was a speculation on the part of Robert Adam, with his brothers James and William, to create a unified residential complex that would include the first architectural embankment of the Thames, with deep arching vaults raising the level of the bank to that of the Strand and supporting symmetrically terraced houses bright with the unique Adam sense of decoration. When finished, it was an immediate sensation. Unfortunately, no one particularly wanted to live in the houses, and they would have remained empty (and the Adams bankrupt) had the adventurous brothers not thought of literally 'raffling off' their work in a lottery. Today one or two bits of the original decorative work can be seen on Adam Street and John Adam Street. The rest was first dressed up in mid-Victorian garb, then later destroyed.

The City of Westminster

By considering what was happening on the Strand in the

Covent Garden Piazza in 1764. No longer a centre of fashion, Covent Garden's main features at this time were its theatres and its market.

Pall Mall East (about 1828) designed by Nash as part of his redevelopment of the West End.

later 18th century, we have of course moved out of the Holborn area into the possessions of the City of Westminster—that immense piece of the heartland of London, which received more benefit than most other areas from the building booms, and which had claimed by that time the high honour of being the most fashionable, most sought-after section of the capital. To a large extent, it has remained so up to our day. It was bounded by Holborn to the east, Marylebone and Paddington to the north, Chelsea and Kensington to the west, the Thames to the south. It was, and remains, the home ground of the monarch and the meeting ground of the Lords and Commons; the container for the low-life of Soho and the high-life of Mayfair; with the green of Regent's Park on its northern extremity and that of St. James's Park on its southern it embraces within its ample confines the culture of the Royal Academy and the National Gallery, the piety of the incomparable Abbey and the milder St. Martin's-in-the-Fields, the history of Trafalgar Square and Parliament Square, the sweeping beauty of The Mall and of Nash's terraces. And it contains, with the exception of certain patches farther north and west, nearly the whole history of London's Regency development.

The migration into and indeed through Westminster in the 18th century can be indicated by developments in two of the best-known areas on its periphery: Covent Garden and Soho. Covent Garden had been exceedingly grand in the 17th century: it retained some grandeur as at least a theatrical centre into Regency times, holding as it did both Drury Lane and the great Opera House. Both of these places have rather sad histories. Young Robert Smirke, the third of the great Regency triumvirate of architects after Nash and Soane, rebuilt the Opera House after it had burned down in 1807. Unhappily it burned again in 1856. Drury Lane had gone through many famous hands—first Wren, then Adam, then Henry Holland—before it was botched by a builder named

Wyatt in 1811, with equally unfortunate additions by others in the 1820s. Some of these ineptitudes can still be seen in the theatre's façade and portico.

But theatres were not enough to keep up Covent Garden's tone. The area's other character, that of a mighty marketplace, undercut the grandeur and allowed tenements, dubious clubs and brothels to creep in and add new dimensions to the night life. Soho, too, had once been a leading residential area—with its 'great square' as the diarist John Evelyn called it—but soon the existing streets fell victim to the crowding and hasty building of lesser areas in the late 18th century, its status not enhanced by encroachments of rougher elements from the Rookery. So the first seeds of Soho's present condition, as the so-called 'sin centre' of modern London, were being sown at the opening of the 19th century.

Similar foretastes of modernity were appearing at that time in Westminster's wealthy residential and shopping area of Mayfair. Unlike more easterly parts of the West End, this section went through an improvement of its character rather than a decline—from the faintly disreputable site of the great annual May Fair itself (which came to an end in the 18th century) and of Edward Shepherd's extensive market to the rich and stately squares and streets being built up in such estates as the Grosvenor. Mayfair's story properly begins with Berkeley Square with its noble homes: Horace Walpole lived in one of them after 1779, surrounded with and delighted by the square's typical quota of aristocrats; and Clive of India had lived and died there. But it was the Grosvenor estate that firmly established Mayfair's nature—laying out its neat gridwork of streets around Grosvenor Square, with immense early Georgian terraces. The encroachment of more streets and houses came from the Piccadilly frontier of the West End, creeping up Bond Street in the beginning, spreading rapidly as the titled residents imposed their cachet on the area.

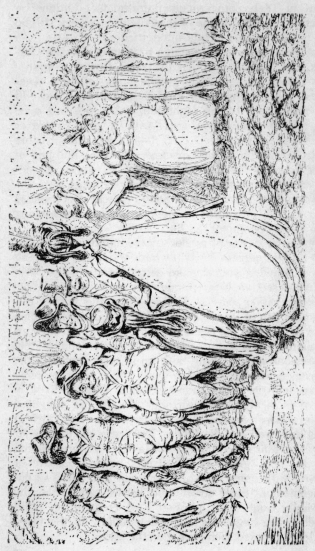

A bizarrely dressed lady provokes a stir in Bond Street (1796). Ladies' fashions were extravagant and extreme—and usually short-lived.

A late 18th-century change in the shopping habits of the rich—whereby the old tradition that the tradesman came to the customer's house gave way to the novelty of the customer, however lordly, visiting the shop—brought an influx of high-class business establishments into Mayfair, and Bond Street became their centre. By that time the street had been extended up to what became Oxford Street, as Mayfair expanded; and it had gained its present twofold nature as Old and New. Top-quality clothiers, chemists, jewellers, bookshops and the like crowded in, spreading off Bond Street into nearby tributaries, completing the creation of Mayfair as a self-contained 'town within a town'. Predominant among the Regency shopping attractions was the elegant Burlington Arcade, a corridor from Piccadilly into the Mayfair interior, lined with tiny gems of shops where even royalty found what it wanted to buy. It was the first of this form of shopping enclosure, which attained vast popularity in the early 1800s; it is just as thronged today. An architect named Ware built it for Lord Cavendish while his lordship was improving the general environs of his Mayfair home, Burlington House. In more recent times the original entrances (and of course the original shop fronts) have been done away with; but a few vestiges of the Regency flavour can still be felt in the Arcade, especially high up towards the top-lighting.

By the time the Prince of Wales performed his transition to the role of the Regent, Mayfair was sprawling westwards to encroach on the vast ducal residences of Park Lane (hardly even a lane, then, and later to become a terrifying traffic bottleneck when the railway age made it a natural thoroughfare between Paddington and Victoria Station). In fact, wealthy or no, neat gridwork of streets or no, Mayfair had its share of uncontrolled growth in three directions. Towards the fourth, southwards, it was balked by the already existing preserves of royalty—the St. James's area. From that courtly centre came the inspiration for a giant new development that was to redesign and reorder not only Mayfair but the whole West End. The Regent was in contact with a middle-aged and reasonably well-off architect named John Nash; the Regent wanted to spend money on a dream of a beautiful royal city to rival Napoleon's Paris —a wish composed in equal parts of 'Prinny's' typical extravagance and a genuine urge to play a part in the age of improvement. The result transformed the City of Westminster.

Regent Street

The spark for the project came from the crown's acquisition of the old Marylebone Park, or Marylebone Fields. Nash, given these lands to work with, began pouring out ideas for redeveloping the Park area, and for constructing a great processional way—a 'Royal Mile'—linking that redevelopment with the St. James's area. (The prince was originally to have a residence in the park, so the new street would connect it with his palace in St. James's. But the royal house in the park never materialised.) To do this, Nash had to carve an avenue of demolition through the heap of second-rate houses that filled the vague borderline between Soho and Mayfair. He also had plans for hacking his way through other built-up quarters in and around St. James's Park, to finish off his creation with a worthy complex of streets at that end.

Every commentator acknowledges that Nash was a great improviser, or in the modern phrase an 'ideas man', who was often found wanting when it came to the taking of infinite practical pains that supposedly characterises genius. It is perhaps just as well, for the sake of whatever individuality and flair there is still remaining of Nash's original work. Even the simple but vastly effective idea of refusing to make Regent Street into a straight line shows something of the man's imaginative quality. He

Buckingham Palace in 1809. Originally built in 1703, it was later much converted by Nash and other architects; Queen Victoria was the first sovereign to live there.

portico has its moments of interest—including the fact that its columns were hand-me-downs from the demolished Carlton House.

Nothing has yet been said about the northern reaches of Nash's great scheme—where, in fact, the first work of the whole began. Though the voluminous plans that he laid down for Regent's Park and its surrounds were never wholly realised, what was created was then and perhaps remains the finest flowering in London of the Regency era's often flashy and never inhibited style. Nash had wanted to fill the Park with gorgeous villas, each with richly planted 'picturesque' grounds. The few that could be managed, in the end, seem paltry; it is not inside the park that one looks for accomplishments. Even the specially cut Regent's Canal, intended to flow through the Park, was disappointingly diverted to its northern fringe. But around the park, in the symmetrical vistas of the great terraces, the Nash dream came into its own. Perhaps some authorities see them as an 'architectural joke'—with the unified frontages looking like mighty mansions but actually disguising rows upon rows of narrow houses—but the unfurling of the whole, to the eyes of a stroller circumnavigating Regent's Park, remains magnificent and palatial in its porticos, arches, and carved pediments.

Nash created Park Crescent just south of the New Road, at first to be part of a new circus, but then as a semicircle to tie in Park Square with a street of imposing houses that the Adams brothers, years before, had constructed—as it were, ready-made for the new Regent Street scheme. This was Portland Place, built in the 1770s in what was then virtually the middle of nowhere —built as a 'close' of mansions, stretching from a nobleman's lordly home to the open fields and farmlands of Marylebone. It fitted without too much difficulty into the early stages of the 'Royal Mile' from the park to St. James's.

Marylebone and St. Pancras

The presence of the Adam buildings on the open land north of the New Road indicates the way in which the West End was growing at the time. A lead would be given by great estates and building complexes, usually owned and lived in by nobility, which would rapidly be caught up by the usual mixed-bag of London buildings— middle-class houses, shops, and the like. Early in the 18th century a few top people had jumped Oxford Road (as it then was) and erected squares and estates in the Marylebone area: the Cavendish and Harley estates (inter- connected by family links) began their development in the 1720s. Cavendish Square is naturally the focal point, as Portman Square is that of the Portman estate farther west. In the wake of these developments of the Georgians' north-west frontier, encouraged by the Adams' work on and around Portland Place, and spurred further by the Regent's Park blossoming, the peaceful parish of St. Marylebone swept into sparkling new life as a major Regency suburb and growth area. It had been helped, in 1783, by the final removal of the notorious Tyburn gallows from its site near what is now Marble Arch—which had always caused Park Lane to be known as 'Tyburn Lane', and Oxford Street as 'Tyburn Road', by the multitudes who went to goggle at the public executions.

But the great Marylebone estates, like the district itself, arose piecemeal. They had had their start in the earliest Georgian days, but the impetus died away; and it took the great moneyed building boom of George III's reign to complete them. Eastwards from their Portland Place, the Adam brothers had put up portions of Fitzroy Square in the 1790s (the piecemeal nature of the times clearly shows in the fact that it was still incomplete after Waterloo). The Adams, naturally, had much else to do with this area: but much of their presence is indirect, through architects who had succumbed to their fashionable influence. Other developments show the trend in Marylebone away from aristocratic estates to a truly urban condition. The presence of Middlesex Hospital (built originally for the healthfulness of the Marylebone fields) lent a professional tone to its vicinity, as did somewhat later the great doctors' precinct of Harley Street. More and more lines of neat, often undeniably plain Georgian houses crept out along the new north-south arteries of Marylebone—especially Baker Street and Wimpole Street. Churches moved in to complete the metamorphosis of the fields into a little town—the imposing St. Marylebone parish church (1818) among them.

The second great building boom, in the early 19th century, filling up the spaces between estates and within estates, caused Marylebone suddenly to find itself crowded. (The Cavendish estate, neatly arranged with fewer than 600 houses in the 1730s, held 9000 by 1806—and the increase continued after Waterloo.) As an overspill, the Bishop of London had speculated on a little estate in the pastoral near-emptiness of Paddington, and in the 1830s more builders began crossing over to join in. (Little of this building is true Georgian; much more of Paddington sprang up when the confident Victorians got their railways running, and the station dragged the city in that direction.) East of Marylebone, John Nash had given a lead with a district (something of an addendum to the Regent's Park plan) of working-class markets and shops east of Albany Street. But by this time the spread of Marylebone was forming a confluence with the northward rush of Bloomsbury into the parish of St. Pancras.

Euston Square had been laid out as the northern outrider of the Bedford Estate that burst into life in Bloomsbury (as seen before) in the early 1800s. Now the space between the Russell Square area and the New Road (Euston Road) filled up rapidly. The area gained some notable publicity in 1830, the year of George IV's death, when a monument to George was erected at King's Cross —a crossroads that had earlier been more romantically known as 'Battle Bridge', after a probably apocryphal ancient battle in which Queen Boadicea claimed a great victory over her enemies. The rather pretentious 1830 monument lasted only 15 years, thanks to a healthy dislike of it (and of the subject, too) among the public. Rather more important to the residents of St. Pancras was the building of their new church, to supplant the little old hamlet chapel that had served since medieval times. The new church got under way in 1819, a fine monumental piece of strict classical architecture—and the worshippers were presumably delighted with the extensive interior ornament, the grand tower, the clever and abundant columns. The committee who had ordered its construction may not have been happy: it is said to have cost £70,000—about four times as much as the average church of its time. And it was a great church-building time.

The Northern Suburbs

The overspill of Marylebone, near the turn of the century, carried London with a rush into the rural north. But again it must be stressed that this movement was not all-encompassing: if the northern extremity of Marylebone led some builders into creating St. John's Wood, and others into invading the arcadian quietude of Hampstead, no one must get the impression that the whole area became suddenly covered with new brick buildings. Huge expanses of fields continued to decorate the northern reaches of London, and to separate these pioneer ventures into Greater London. It might be added that this leapfrog expansion did no good to these intervening patches of greensward, as Charles Dickens later made clear (the patchwork nature of north London having lasted till then) when writing about a residential area near the Finchley Road:

'It is neither of the town nor country. The former, like the giant in his travelling boots, has made a stride and passed it, and has set his brick-and-mortar heel a long way in advance; but the intermediate space between the giant's feet, as yet, is only blighted country, and not town, and here, among a few tall chimneys belching smoke all day and night, and among the brickfields and lanes where turf is cut, and where the fences tumble down, and where the dusty nettles grow, and where a scrap or two of hedge may yet be seen, and where the bird-catcher still comes occasionally, though he swears every time to come no more—this home is to be found.'

What is often thought, if rarely so well expressed, by exurbanites in today's Green Belt dormitory towns.

The Eyre Estate led the movement into what is now St. John's Wood (which had been, long before, actual forest). This estate deserves remembering above all for a startling innovation in its plans. It was to be composed primarily of villas, with ample lands and gardens—as opposed to the usual shoulder-to-shoulder neighbourliness of terraces. But some of the villas emerged as semi-detached houses—which goes down in London's history as the first occurrence of this now traditional use of the 'semi' in a residential development. St. John's Wood itself came to be built up mainly in the 1820s and 30s; but the original plans for the villas, semis and all, go back as far as 1794.

Hampstead had received its first incursions much earlier—in Queen Anne's day, and to some extent even before—when city builders profited by the speculative building of modest country houses for merchants and professional men. These houses came mostly in the form of terraces, with varying degrees of size and spaciousness, but there was a considerable scattering later of attractive villas. Towards the end of the 18th century, and in Regency times, the popularity of Hampstead (due to its hilltop vistas, its lovely wild heath, and its abundance of young artists and poets who clustered round Leigh Hunt) caused it to expand to the more remote parts of the parish—the Pond Street area, to the North End and so on. Men who like Keats felt 'in city pent' convinced themselves they had moved to the country by taking up residence in this civilised, wealthy suburb—but more usually they merely brought the city to Hampstead with them.

Highgate had felt the incursions of these early suburbanites rather less than Hampstead, being less immediately accessible from the West End. But it had had its share of speculative house-building, and by the turn of the century the villas-for-the-tired-City-business-men motif had stretched out even to Hornsey and Crouch Hill. Meanwhile, country villages closer to London were decidedly feeling the shadow of the metropolis. Camden Town had been built up in an earlier estate development, with terraces along the Hampstead Road; and St. Pancras was pouring into the spaces between. Kentish Town, still rural when Leigh Hunt moved there in the 1820s, had for some time been a favourite summering place for lower middle-class Londoners who could not afford country houses; where lodging houses and middling shops arose, there soon followed the rest of the array of a true suburb. East of that area, however, the City of London had been spreading its tentacles for nearly a century.

Islington

The 17th century, as has been noted, showed the first extensive signs of the migration of people out of the City, and of its eventual demise as a residential area. Islington had felt the effects of this shift even then, so that by the 18th century it had been well launched on its evolution (or, depending on the point of view, decline) from village into suburb. Terraces had moved out northwards along its main roads, and had bred more built-up areas on linking roads. By the 1780s the waves of brown brick had reached Highbury, and were still rolling on. For some time, though, much of Islington and its environs retained a rural flavour, in the 'backwoods' away from the central flurries of building: village life retained its character around Islington Green, and Charles Lamb could still walk across fields, in the 1800s, from his home near the Angel. But soon the Regency estate-building fever caught up with Islington, led especially by the Canonbury Estate. Most of these north-eastern estates lack both the splendour and the style of the West End estates, and were inhabited principally by business and professional men rather than the nobility. But the Canonbury enclave remains one of the most interestingly planned and unpretentiously attractive segments of Islington's large share of late Georgian architecture.

South-west Suburbs

Though Regency London's greatest sprawl took place in the north and west, it was not entirely unbalanced by developments in the opposite direction. Above all, the bulging City of Westminster rapidly pushed its way south-west, into Belgravia. This area had gained in importance by the Regent's designation of old Buckingham House as his new palace-to-be, and the speculators rushed in. Belgrave Square was begun in 1825 as a nucleus of this development, and boasts some worthy examples of the classical Regency style—the dwellings, true to the nature of Westminster, of the titled. These houses were mostly built in blocks, as was usual around the square, but three separate mansions also rose grandly on three corners. The entirety of the Belgravia complex was designed with a careful eye for layout and planning (not always present among the rushed and flamboyant Regency builders). Its speculator-builder, Thomas Cubitt, took the same care in later years when he applied himself to expanding Belgravia into the Pimlico area. By then another self-contained estate had grown up on the west fringe of Belgravia, called Hans Town, its main arteries being Sloane Street and Cadogan Place.

This extension meant that Chelsea had come into the metropolitan embrace. That pleasant little country village of earlier years had already been threatened by the usual lines of houses thrusting out along important roads (like the King's Road), and had been invaded to some extent by the rural retreats of wealthy Londoners (as with Hampstead). Such houses had in fact reached Fulham, and had begun to occur in such truly countrified depths as Richmond and Twickenham. Knightsbridge and Kensington were captured by greater London at this time too, with suburban terraces along Kensington Gore, and builders rushing in to claim sites towards Hammersmith. As, indeed, they were in just about every other village within a ten-mile radius of central London.

Areas south of the river were not at all left out of the picture. Dulwich had become a favourite suburban residential area for City men: Nash was among the leading architects who busily designed villas there, paralleling the developments in St. John's Wood and north London. Battersea, Streatham, Wandsworth and Camberwell were among the southern areas suffering the arrival of the city's advance guard—terraces and villas—in the 18th century. Some became reasonably fashionable, in Dulwich's manner; others just became built up and populated. Clapham received some fine terraces on its North Side, and Belgravia's Cubitt turned his expertise into that area to lay out some pleasant streets. The road from Blackfriars Bridge into Lambeth, new in George III's time, had by the time of George IV brought a major build-up of terraces into that giant parish—which gained extra esteem by a wave of church-building that swept through it after Waterloo.

By the 1830s, many people (including leading architects and planners as well as crusty traditionalists) felt that London had grown far enough, or too far. One optimistic planner, indeed, tried to interest the authorities in a plan for the western parts of Westminster that were based on literally containing the city, so that it should not expand past Hyde Park. Few of these men could have guessed at the extent to which the Victorians would contract the late Georgian fever for improvement and for speculation. And, fortunately for their happiness, few foresaw how extensively the word 'improvement' would be defined in Victorian terms as 'tearing down Georgian'. It is true, though, that a fair portion of later Georgian construction lacked the solidity and permanence we might have wished: speculation and expansionism tend to lead to some shoddiness, however good the intentions. Our century knows this all too well—and the Regency builders' efforts have also suffered gravely at 20th-century hands. One need point only to the current (1968) rape of Georgian Bloomsbury. Yet there are still fragments of the great Adam days and the perhaps greater Nash days standing here and there around the city. Perhaps if enough people could be made aware of them, could be induced to look at them, they might be with us a while longer. To that end the next chapter is dedicated.

Regency London: What remains

Some indications have already been given previously about trends in building styles during the period 1760–1837. These can be expanded a little here, as guidelines for anyone who intends to go and look at buildings.

No one manner of building predominated during all of these 77 years, for British architects have always been noted for their individualism, and never so much as during the Regency. So the most practical way to make the accessible architectural approaches to the time must be to look at the architects, and their styles—and to look at them in terms of both their public buildings and their private houses. Broadly speaking, the period splits neatly into two: the heyday of the Adams, in George III's reign, and that of Nash in the Regency. Coexistent with Adam were such important competitors as James Wyatt, Sir William Chambers and later Henry Holland; Nash's eminence was shared (if not topped) by Sir John Soane, with the younger Robert Smirke and Thomas Cubitt rising rapidly.

The Palladian style, as has been indicated, rested on

the solid base of classicism. It forced its way into the British consciousness in the 17th century, when the Italian travels of Inigo Jones filled his head with Roman forms—with attendant rules of proportion and requirements of extra features (columns, capitals, and so on). By mid-Georgian times Palladianism had also filled London. And it is important to remember that no architects of importance broke away, in any drastic fashion, from the Palladian mood until the 19th century. It was not a fashion, but the norm: any deviations from it, such as that of Adam, were fashions—and generally could be found mainly in the excrescences, the approach to decoration or to surface features. In other words, the architecture within the Adam-to-Nash period can be seen as a series of variations on the Palladian theme, not as a total breakdown of the theme. Classical proportion and precision remained the watchwords, insofar as the architects were skilful enough to achieve these ends.

Robert Adam's inventiveness came along to free architecture from the crippling effects of too many rules too rigidly followed (much as the better poets of George III's reign, like Gray or Goldsmith, reacted away from the inhibitions of the heroic couplet, then blunted and worn from over-use, without actually staging a revolt against 18th-century neo-classicism). Adam reinvigorated the norm, without basically departing too far from it. Where Palladian buildings had become stiff and dull, he made their lines flow and move; where they had become tediously plain, he gave them colour and glitter. Georgian architecture had come to speak in clichés; Adam gave it freshness and originality. If in the process it learned to speak with perhaps over-precious affectation, we must remember not to blame the master for all the failings of his disciples. Yet within all this novelty, the Graeco-Roman basis stayed solid: Adam's buildings may have had some bizarre moments, may have had stucco smeared over their good plain English brick—but the columns and porticos and arches still were there to gladden traditionalists. And the work of Chambers, Palladian and conservative to the core, departed in practically no way from the norm.

Nash, however, did depart from it in rather more ways than his predecessors. Adam had opened a door, Nash moved through it. He used stucco much more extensively; he played with façades and frontages, making them 'busy' and moving, in a way that left the classical rules governing these features in shards at his feet. He picked up Adam's wide use of plaster in such things as decorative pilasters (supports, often columnar, attached to walls) and extended it to newer uses. In Nash's time the Roman dominance within Palladianism gave way to more graceful, harmonious Greek forms. And Nash broke more rules, by mixing his metaphors, patching a bit of Roman on to a piece of Greek, not averse to throwing in some semi-digested oriental influence as well. Yet the principles of proportion that characterised Georgian buildings never entirely left his drawing board (or, if they did, it was because of his natural sloppiness rather than any urge to total innovation).

Finally, before getting on to a sampling of individual buildings, a note on public architecture and private. Non-architects may not make a great deal out of writings about 'proportion' and 'mass relationships', but their eyes will be able to discern something of the interconnections between height and breadth, between the position and size of doors and windows, and in the arrangement of the various external features such as decorative sculpture on public buildings, or the entablatures and cornices that surmount all those classical columns. These relationships should be looked for in spite of the generally overpowering classical accretions of public buildings and great houses, especially the Graeco-Roman porticos (the usual centrepiece of the frontage) with their colonnades and surmounting pediments. The Greek revival in the

Regency, bringing this sort of frontage to an extreme, might be sampled by looking at Downing College, Cambridge—or at the fantastic colonnaded façade of the British Museum, 44 Ionic columns and a mighty pediment that have never seemed entirely connected with the building behind it, however many ponderous wings have been added.

So the classical decorations and imposing features of façades may often divert the eye from the purity and proportion of the overall design, in the stately homes and dignified public buildings. Often the diversion became an intentional disguise, as with Nash's desire to make his Regent's Park terraces of tall, narrow houses look, from a distance, like individual palaces. But with lesser houses, mostly also in terraces, simplicity allows the Georgian purity to shine through. Sometimes, indeed, the simplicity devolves into plainness, into monotony, of the kind that so irritated the Victorians and led them to react into overloads of frippery (and to demolish Georgian houses). But the quiet, smooth elegance of typical George III terrace houses, in plain brick, with subtle and restrained ornamentations around the door and windows, and perhaps a wrought-iron balcony across the first floor windows—or the variants on this theme, stucco on the brick, columns or pilasters setting off the doorway, decorous pediments above the windows, sometimes the well-known Regency bowed windows (frequent in the shopfronts). All these elements at their best form themselves into harmonious arrangements, directing the onlooker's eye to a grasp of the entirety of the composition, the balance and the symmetry.

Where possible, more particular details will be provided concerning the buildings—public and private—in the selection that follows of extant Georgian architecture. They are arranged by area, rather than by chronology or by architect, to assist in their accessibility to the discoverer of London.

Bloomsbury and Holborn

British Museum. Not the most representative piece of Regency architecture, but certainly the dominant feature of the area. Built by Robert Smirke between 1823 and 1847, on the site of Old Montagu House (which had held the early Museum collections since 1759). Note especially the King's Library interior, with its serene spaciousness and subtle handling of columns and decorations. (The Museum's Reading Room and a great many galleries were added after the close of the Regency period.)

How to get there: the great southern colonnade of the Museum faces onto Great Russell Street; Montague Street runs along its eastern side. Underground to Tottenham Court Road. Buses: 1, 14, 24, 29, 73, etc. southbound on Gower Street, 19, 38, 38A eastbound on New Oxford Street.

Pharmaceutical Society building, Bloomsbury Square. A solid and unpretentious building designed by Nash in the 1770s, with interesting use of pilasters and typical Nash stucco on the front. On the north-west corner of the square. Underground to Holborn. Buses 19, 38, 38A eastbound on New Oxford Street.

Stone Buildings, Lincoln's Inn. Built by Sir Robert Taylor in the 1770s, with a clean Palladian strength in the main façades, and some original approaches to ornament. They suffered some damage during the war, but the original fabric remains intact. Underground to Holborn. Buses 7, 8, 22, 23, 25 to High Holborn; 171 northbound on Chancery Lane. (The compound of Lincoln's Inn is open to the public during normal weekday office hours.)

Lincoln's Inn Fields. A good many fine buildings still stand round the circumference of the beautiful gardens— above all the house of Sir John Soane and its neighbours on the north side of the fields. Soane's house (which he completed in 1812) is now a museum, with its interior and furnishings either the originals or accurate copies. Space does not permit a full account of the riches, the glories, the fantasies contained in this eccentric architect's house; there is a super-abundance of vases, busts, urns, plasters, fragments of antique marble and more. There are paintings by Reynolds, Lawrence, and Hogarth and a host of sculptures, plaques and other *objets d'art* gathered by Soane. The furniture is beautifully 18th-century, the layout of the rooms authentic, the staircases and passages typical and worth close study. The decorated ceilings are breathtaking. The whole—if such a feast can ever be seen as a whole—might well be alone the best introduction to Regency buildings and Regency life, if it were not for the extravagance, the tendency to the bizarre, that can be seen in Soane as interior decorator and collector (though rarely seen in Soane as architect). The museum also contains Soane's sizeable collection of books and architectural drawings, accessible to students. The house is open to the public 10 am to 5 pm, Tuesday to Saturday. Underground and buses as for Stone Buildings, above; buses also 68, 77, 170, 172, etc. on Kingsway.

Bedford Square. Perhaps the most impressive of the Bloomsbury–St. Pancras unified squares; built in the 1770s, no specific designer is credited. Some Adamesque touches on many of the houses; note also the 'Coade stone' doorways (a special composition material whose basic ingredients remained a secret throughout the widespread use of it in late Georgian building). No. 1, Bedford Square, is a separate construction, standing out from the rest of the square's uniformity. Underground to Tottenham Court Road. Buses 1, 14, 24, 29, 73, etc. southbound on Gower Street.

Tavistock, Woburn, Russell, Mecklenburgh and many

other north Bloomsbury squares retain some features of their Georgian construction. Mecklenburgh, a quiet backwater off Guilford Street, has been largely rebuilt since the Second World War, but in a reasonable facsimile of its original appearance. Underground to Russell Square. Buses 17, 18, 45 on Gray's Inn Rd. Tavistock, Woburn and Russell Squares, underground to Russell Square station; buses 68, 77, 188, 196 on Woburn Place (Southampton Row).

Doughty Street. A continuation of John Street, and one of those uniform streets of exceptional plain, simple frontages that made the Victorians mutter about 'monotony'. Underground to Russell Square or Chancery Lane. Buses 19, 38, 170, 172 on Theobald's Road.

St. Pancras Church. Built by the Inwoods, father and son, 1818–22. Has been described as simply a great hall, with an apse at one end and a vestibule, tower and portico at the other. But it neatly solved the nagging Georgian problem of combining a tower with a portico by a subtle use of recessed columns. The interior has a flat ceiling, not ornamented. Underground to Euston Square. Buses 14, 18, 30, 73, 77, 196 on Euston Road.

Westminster

Somerset House. Built by Sir William Chambers, 1776–86 (see Chapter 3); Robert Smirke added the east wing, 1828–34. One of the better remaining examples of ponderous and dignified Georgian public architecture. Underground to Aldwych. Buses 9, 11, 13, 15, 60, 77, etc. to the Strand.

John Adam Street. The Royal Society of Arts building is one of the few portions of Robert Adam's Adelphi still intact. Visits by appointment only. Underground to Strand or Charing Cross stations. Buses as for Somerset House.

Trafalgar Square. The square's layout was of course Nash's, as mentioned in Chapter 3. Its north side contains the National Gallery, the original work of 1834–38 still visible in spite of many additions. Underground to Trafalgar Square; buses as for Somerset House, above; also 1, 24, 29, 134, etc. on Charing Cross Road; also 3, 11, 12, and more on Whitehall.

Admiralty. The screen across the Admiralty courtyard was one of Robert Adam's first commissions (1760). Its object was simply to cover, literally to screen off, the awkward and unsuccessful façade of the older building. Underground and buses as for Trafalgar Square.

Haymarket Theatre. The present grand Corinthian portico of the theatre was given to it by Nash in 1820, and was intended to close off the vista from St. James's Square, along Charles II Street. It was one of his side-steps during the construction of the Regent Street project. Underground Piccadilly; buses 14, 19, 22, 38 southbound on the Haymarket.

St. James's Street. One or two late 18th-century shop-fronts stand out along this key Regency street, which also contains some leading clubs—including Brooks's and Boodle's—that have lasted from that time. Underground to Green Park station; buses northbound as for Haymarket.

Pall Mall. More famous clubs, erected in the early 19th century: the Athenaeum and Travellers' were both built 1829–32. Nash built the United Services club, but it was later altered by a Victorian architect. Underground and buses as for St. James's Street.

Carlton House Terraces. Nash's attempt to offset the loss of Carlton House, the southern kingpin of his Regent

Street scheme. These typical Nash terraces have undergone a good deal of damage, neglect and alteration, but remain worth seeing as part of the overall plan. It is also true that they reveal Nash's slapdash methods—for while the idea of the sweep of Corinthian columns was a good one, some of the detail seems unbalanced and more than a little contrived. Underground and buses as for St. James's Street.

Albany. The central block was built by Chambers as a town home for Lord Melbourne in 1770—the usual restrained Palladianism of Chambers being very apparent in its brown brick façade. Some of the residential blocks were added in 1804 by Holland, who also laid out its forecourt. Underground to Piccadilly Circus; buses 9, 14, 19, 22, 25, 38 along Piccadilly.

Burlington Arcade. Built by Samuel Ware 1815–19. For admirers of the Regency whose imaginations can overcome modern shop windows and up-dated entrances, it remains still one of the best instant means of transport back to that time. (And its shops still cater for the same class of people as in its beginnings.) Underground and buses as for Albany.

Hyde Park. The screen and the arch at Hyde Park Corner were both built (from 1825) by a bright young architect named Decimus Burton, and stood on the same axis—so that the Ionic screen provided an attractive introduction to the more massive structure of the arch. Inexplicably, the Victorians ignored this intention, and in 1888 rebuilt the arch to face the approach of Constitution Hill, wrecking the relationship of the two and creating a monumental awkwardness not enhanced by the Edwardian rubbish set on top of the arch in 1912. Underground to Hyde Park Corner; buses 9, 14, 19, 22, 38 to Hyde Park Corner.

the Hans Town development, which can be sought on *Cadogan Place* and *Hans Place*, this street offers one of the tidiest rows of early 19th-century houses (with one or two shops) in the borough. Underground to South Kensington station (then walk down Onslow Square). Buses: 49 to Sydney Street; 14, 45 on Fulham Road; 11, 19, 22 on King's Road.

Hampstead: *Holly Bush Hill* retains a few delightful late 18th-century houses, and *Mount Vernon* has a terrace from the early 1800s. Underground to Hampstead. *Keats Grove* has several beautiful little houses from about 1815, brick or stucco and a wide variation in appearance—as well as the added attraction of the restored *Keats House*. Underground to Hampstead station (walk down High Street, turn onto Downshire Hill); buses 24, 45, 187 to South End Road.

Highgate: *Kenwood*. A lordly country house with a considerable history before the Earl of Mansfield commissioned Robert Adam to remodel it in the 1760s. Adam erected a towering portico, with a glowing pediment, on the north front; the south front, overlooking the gardens, has much of the free flowing 'movement' that Adam was determined to inject into the petrified body of Palladianism. Later, in the 1790s, the next earl added white-brick wings to the house that contributed little to the unity of the façade, since Adam had stuccoed his part. But the servants' wing, added at the same time as the other wings, is pleasantly inconspicuous and notable for its richly brown bricks. When Kenwood was finally saved from destruction by the philanthropy of the Earl of Iveagh in the 1920s, much of its furnishings had been disposed of—but the house is today furnished in a contemporary style that makes it a worthy mirror of upperclass Georgian life. It is the interior decoration, however, that remains unforgettable. Kenwood was one of Adam's first essays in the use of colour for decor: and the elegant ceiling of the entrance hall, the breathtaking design of the library's curved ceiling, are among his finest accomplishments—a 'harlequinade', in another of Sacheverell Sitwell's just phrases.

Kenwood is open to the public from 10 am weekdays (2 pm Sundays) until 4 pm in winter, 7 pm in summer. No nearby underground; 210 bus from Archway or Golders Green station.

Museums to visit

The British Museum

Address:	Great Russell Street, W.C.1
Admission:	Free
Opening hours:	Monday—Saturday: 10 am—5 pm
	Sundays: 2.30 pm—6 pm
Closed:	Christmas Day and Good Friday
	Open Bank Holidays usual hours
Access:	

By Underground:
Tottenham Court Road (Central & Northern Lines)—
turn right along Tottenham Court Road and right at
Great Russell Street. Museum on left. Russell Square
(Piccadilly Line)—left out of station, cross Russell
Square, and left on Montague Street to Great Russell
Street and main entrance of Museum.

By Bus:
77, 68, 188, 196, to Southampton Row. Turn left along
Great Russell Street. 73 to Tottenham Court Road/
Oxford Street. Right along Great Russell Street.
7, 8, 23, 25, to Bloomsbury Way. Turn along Museum
Street (from West).
7, 8, 22, 23, 25, from Holborn direction. Alight at High
Holborn, just past Kingsway, and cross road, along Drury
Lane or Grape Street, cross New Oxford Street and con-
tinue along Coptic Street or Museum Street.

By Car:
Drive from West along Oxford Street, turn left at Tot-
tenham Court Road, and right almost immediately at
Great Russell Street.
From East, along Holborn to Kingsway, turn right along
Southampton Row, and left at Great Russell Street.
N.B. There is limited parking at the Museum—otherwise,
at east side in Montague Street/Russell Square.

The British Museum, in a partly Regency building, also contains a fine Regency collection. It is mostly composed of antiquities and art objects—ivories, enamelware, silverware, glassware and the like—as well as manuscripts of major Regency poets in the Manuscript Room.

The Victoria and Albert Museum

Address : South Kensington, S.W.7
Admission : Free
Opening hours : Monday—Saturday : 10 am—6 pm
  Sundays : 2.30 pm—6 pm
Closed : Christmas Day and Good Friday
  Open Bank Holidays usual hours
Access :

By Underground:
South Kensington (District, Circle and Piccadilly Lines)—a subway connects the station and the museum, giving entrance on N.W. (Exhibition Road) side. Main entrance to museum is on Cromwell Road.

By Bus:
207, 45, 49, to South Kensington Station. 14, 30, 74, to Brompton Oratory, at junction of Brompton Road and Cromwell Road.
The Victoria and Albert Museum possesses a vast collection of prints, drawings and paintings from the period, and of course also art objects such as pottery, porcelain, metalwork. And it offers wide-ranging displays of Regency costume and furniture.

The London Museum

Address: Kensington Palace, Kensington
                        Gardens, W.8
Admission: Free
Opening hours: 1 March—30 September:
                        10 am—6 pm (Sundays: 2 pm—6 pm)
                        1 October—28 February:
                        10 am—4 pm (Sundays: 2 pm—4 pm)
Closed: Good Friday, Christmas Eve, and
                        Christmas Day
Access:

By Underground:

Queensway (Central Line)—cross Bayswater Road and walk through Broad Walk in Kensington Gardens to Palace. Kensington High Street (Circle and District Line from Earls Court to Edgware Road)—turn right along Kensington High Street to Park. Left through Park to Palace.

By Bus:

12, 88, along Bayswater Road to Queensway, then as above from Queensway Station.
9, 46, 52, 73, to Palace Gate in Kensington Road. Walk through Park to Palace.

By Car:

The best place to park is in the squares and side streets off Bayswater Road or Kensington Road. Then walk through Park.

The London Museum must be an essential stopping place for all discoverers of London, for it is devoted entirely to the history of the city. There is an immense number of prints and drawings, as well as fine porcelain, silverware and perhaps the best array of Regency costume that can be seen anywhere.

The Wallace Collection

Address: Manchester Square, W.1
Admission: Free
Opening hours: Weekdays: 10 am—5 pm
                      Sundays: 2 pm—5 pm
Closed: Good Friday, Christmas Eve, and
                      Christmas Day
Access:

By Underground:
Bond Street Station (Central Line); Baker Street Station
(Bakerloo & District Lines).

By Bus:
2, 13, 23, 30, 59, 59a, 74, 113, 153, 159 to Portman Square;
6, 7, 7a, 8, 12, 15, 17, 23a, 60, 73, 88, 137 to Selfridges.
The Wallace Collection offers an extensive look at the
furniture of the period, and also has a wide sampling of
Georgian art and craftsmanship.

The Geffrye Museum

Address: Kingsland Road, Shoreditch, E.2
Admission: Free
Opening hours: Tuesday—Saturday: 10 am—5 pm
                     Sundays: 2 pm—5 pm
Closed: Mondays, except Bank Holidays,
                     Christmas Day
Access:

By Underground:
Liverpool St. (Metropolitan and Central London Lines)
and Old St. (Northern).

By Bus:
22, 35, 36, 47, 67, 78, 149, 170, 243, 256, 257. Alight at
Kingsland Road (Pearson Street request stop).
The Geffrye Museum (which is contained in Georgian
almshouses dating from 1751) houses a series of typically
furnished and decorated rooms, many of which are from
the 18th and 19th century. Also ironwork and some
period shop fronts.

The National Maritime Museum

Address: Romney Road, Greenwich, S.E.10
Admission: Free
Opening hours: Weekdays: 10 am—6 pm
                   Sundays: 2.30 pm—6 pm
Closed: Christmas Day and Good Friday
Access:

By Train:
Charing Cross, Waterloo, London Bridge or Cannon Street to Maze Hill, five minutes' walk from Museum. More frequent trains to New Cross, with bus on to Greenwich.

By Bus:
70 from London Bridge; 163 and 177 from Westminster Bridge; 53 from Westminster; 180 from Catford; 185 from Victoria; 188 from Waterloo.

By River (in summer):
Direct motor launch from Westminster Pier to Greenwich.

The National Maritime Museum presents the history of Britain's rise as a great sea power—including many relics of Nelson and the Battle of Trafalgar.

The Science Museum

Address: Exhibition Road, South Kensington,
                         S.W.7
Admission: Free
Opening hours: Weekdays: 10 am—6 pm
                         Sundays: 2.30 pm—6 pm
Closed: Christmas Day and Good Friday
Access:

By Underground:
South Kensington Station (District and Piccadilly Lines)
is a few minutes' walk from the Museum.

By Bus:
9, 46, 52, 73, via Kensington High Street or Knightsbridge. 14, 30, 45, 49, 74, 96, via Brompton Road or South
Kensington Station.
The Science Museum holds a fine collection of Georgian
and Regency mechanical artefacts, including clocks and
watches, and many examples of the period's means of
transport. But above all it has representations (and sometimes working models) of early machinery that introduced the Industrial Revolution.

The Wellington Museum

Address: Hyde Park Corner
Admission: 1s. (children 6d.)
Opening hours: Weekdays: 10 am—6 pm
                   Sundays: 2.30 pm—6 pm
Closed: Good Friday and Christmas Day
Access:

By Underground:
Hyde Park Corner (Piccadilly Line).

By Bus:
2, 9, 14, 16, 19, 22, 25, 30, 36, 38, 52, 73, 74, 137 to Hyde Park Corner.
The Wellington Museum (in Apsley House, remodelled by Wyatt) contains a collection of relics, memorabilia and works of art relating to or once belonging to the 'Iron Duke'.

The National Gallery

Address:	Trafalgar Square, W.C.2
Admission:	Free
Opening hours:	Weekdays: 10 am—6 pm
	Sundays: 2 pm—6 pm
	June-September, inclusive, open till 9 pm on Tuesdays and Thursdays
Closed:	Christmas Eve, Christmas Day, and Good Friday
Access:	

By Underground:
Trafalgar Square (Bakerloo Line), Leicester Square (Piccadilly Line), Strand (Northern Line).

By Bus:
1, 3, 6, 9, 11, 12, 13, 15, 24, 29, 39, 53a, 59, 59a, 60, 77, 77a, 88, 96, 134, 153, 159.

The National Gallery has, naturally, the original collection given to the nation by the Regent—and also contains fine works by Turner and other major painters and sculptors of the period. At the same time, one can see the nearby National Portrait Gallery, with portraits of famous people from the 16th century till now.

Special museums relating to the late Georgian period alone, which have already been mentioned (in Chapter 4): Sir John Soane Museum, Lincoln's Inn Fields; Keats' House and Museum, Keats' Grove; Kenwood (the Iveagh Bequest), Hampstead Lane.

Who's Who in Regency London

George III (1738–1820): grandson of George II, reigned from 1760 until his always incipient madness became permanent in 1811.

George IV (1762–1830): Prince Regent from 1811, king from 1820. Though often scorned in his time and since for his grossness, extravagance, childishness and dissoluteness—and for creating in British minds at the time a hearty dislike of royalty—he nevertheless was a man of acute taste and wide discernment, who contributed much to the style and artistry of his time.

William IV (1765–1837): brother of George IV, he occupied the throne (1830–37) but did little to fill it; upon his death the *Spectator* stated flatly that he had been 'a weak, ignorant, commonplace sort of person'.

William Pitt the elder (later Earl of Chatham) (1708–1778): one of the greatest Georgian statesmen—powerful parliamentarian, popular war leader, domineering administrator, and so frequently an opponent of the crown and an enemy to other powerful Whigs that he was in and out of power regularly till his death.

William Pitt the younger (1759–1806): with much of the political acumen of his father, served as first lord of the treasury twice, each time pushing forward the cautious but definite principles of reform to which he subscribed.

Robert Clive (later Baron Clive of Plessey) (1725–1774): leading British general whose victorious campaigns in India against French-controlled Indian princes (in the 1750s) opened the door for Britain's massive rush to Empire.

Tom Paine (1737–1809): English-born but widely travelled, perhaps the greatest political revolutionary until Lenin—whose writings and political thinking infused true radical fire into both the American and the French revolutions. Author among other works of the seminal *Rights of Man*.

Horatio (later Viscount) Nelson (1758–1805): the admiral who gave Britain a hero when she desperately needed one, in the darkest days of the French war—and whose victory at Trafalgar awoke the world to a realisation of Britain's maritime dominance.

Duke of Wellington (formerly Arthur Wellesley) (1769–1852): the victor at Waterloo, who made up in courage and determination what he lacked in military flair and imagination. Later first lord of the treasury, at which these virtues proved less useful.

Sir Robert Peel (1788–1850): dominant in politics in the early 19th century, as home secretary from 1822 lent his name and his power to furthering the spirit of reform then catching fire across the country. First lord of the treasury twice after 1834.

John Nash (1752–1835): the man whose name leaps to mind as consonant with 'Regency architecture'—though in fact no more important architecturally, and possibly less talented as a builder, than Sir John Soane (1753–1837). Nash, however, will always be remembered for his huge essay in town planning that gave later generations the joy of the Regent's Park terraces.

Further reading list

R. Bayne-Powell   *Eighteenth-Century London Life*, John Murray

Boris Ford (Editor)   *From Blake to Byron* (*Pelican Guide to English Literature*), Penguin Books

M. D. George   *London Life in the Eighteenth Century*, Penguin Books

W. L. Mathieson   *England in Transition 1789–1832*, Longmans, Green

R. J. Mitchell and M. D. R. Leys   *A History of London Life*, Longmans, Green

Nikolaus Pevsner   *The Buildings of England: London* (vols i and ii), Penguin Books

Donald Pilcher   *The Regency Style*, Batsford

J. H. Plumb   *England in the Eighteenth Century 1714–1815* (*Pelican History of England*), Penguin Books

J. H. Plumb   *The First Four Georges*, Fontana Books

M. and C. H. B. Quennell   *History of Everyday Things in England*, part iii, Batsford

Paul Reilly   *Regency Architecture*, Ed. H. Casson

A. E. Richardson   *Introduction to Georgian Architecture*, Art and Technics Ltd.

Sacheverell Sitwell   *British Architects and Craftsmen*, Pan Books

J. Summerson   *Georgian London* (revised edition), Penguin Books

David Thomson   *Europe since Napoleon*, Penguin Books

G. M. Trevelyan	*English Social History*, Penguin Books
J. S. Watson	*The Reign of George III* (*Oxford History of England*, vol xii), Oxford University Press
E. L. Woodward	*The Age of Reform* (*Oxford History of England*, vol xiii), Oxford University Press

Discovering London

Other Books in the Series

This volume is one of a set of eight books that trace the growth of London from Roman times to the end of Queen Victoria's reign. The other books are:

Set One

Set Two

Each title is available separately, price 6s. Alternatively each set of four volumes is available in box with a special fold-out map of the area, price 25s.